LIKE BREAD, THEIR VOICES RISE!

Sr. Francis Bernard O'Connor spent twenty years working in Bangladesh prior to serving as Regional Superior for the overseas ministry of the Sisters of the Holy Cross. From 1984-1989 she was Superior General of her congregation. She is presently a Research Scholar at the Kellogg Institute for International Studies at the University of Notre Dame.

LIKE BREAD, THEIR VOICES RISE!

Global Women Challenge the Church

SR. FRANCIS BERNARD O'CONNOR, C.S.C.

AVE MARIA PRESS   NOTRE DAME, INDIANA 46556

Acknowledgments

Excerpts of "A Psalm in Praise of Anonymous Women," "Prayer," "A Psalm for Women Who Weep," and "A Liberation Psalm for Women" are from *Woman-Word*, copyright © 1990 by Miriam Therese Winter, The Crossroad Publishing Company, New York, NY. Used by permission.

Excerpts of "A Psalm for Those Passed Over," and "A Psalm Celebrating a Royal Priesthood" are from *WomanWitness*, copyright © 1992 by Miriam Therese Winter, The Crossroad Publishing Company, New York, NY. Used by permission.

Excerpts of "A Psalm for Keeping Faith," "A Psalm of Confidence," "A Psalm for Shedding Pretenses," "Because-I-Am-a-Woman," "A Psalm of Wise Words," and "A Psalm of Freedom" are from *WomanWisdom*, copyright © 1991 by Miriam Therese Winter, The Crossroad Publishing Company, New York, NY. Used by permission.

Excerpts of "I Am a Woman Weaver" are from *Crossing the Lines*, by Marsie Silvestro, copyright © 1987 by MoonSong Productions/Marsie Silvestro, Cambridge, MA. Used by permission.

Excerpt from *Gitanjali* by Rabindranath Tagore, translated by Brother James Talarovic, copyright © 1983 University Press Limited, Dhaka, Bangladesh. Used by permission.

Excerpt from *Gitanjali* by Rabindranath Tagore, copyright © 1971 Collier Books/Macmillan, New York, NY. Reprinted with permission of Macmillan Publishing Company.

Excerpt from "Litany of the Bread" from *Our Passion for Justice: Images of Power, Sexuality, and Liberation*, by Carter Heyward, copyright © 1984 The Pilgrim Press, Cleveland, OH. Used by permission.

Unless otherwise noted, scripture selections from **The New American Bible With Revised New Testament** Copyright © 1986 by the Confraternity of Christian Doctrine, Washington, DC, are all used with permission of the copyright owner. All rights reserved.

International Standard Book Number: 0-87793-509-2

Library of Congress Catalog Card Number: 93-77734

Cover and text design by Katherine Robinson Coleman

Cover and inside illustrations by Birdie R. McElroy

Printed and bound in the United States of America.

CONTENTS

To anonymous women everywhere . . .
For all those women unnamed and unknown
in the course of human history,
anonymous women, invisible women,
unidentified and unrecorded women.
We remember you now and we praise you.
Anonymous women everywhere, of every
culture and every class
every religion and every race,
from the beginning of time to this time and place,
especially those who are in our midst.
All who were labeled "the daughters of men" . . .
by those who were labeled "the sons of God" . . .
Rejoice now as we praise you![1]
I dedicate this book to you.

ACKNOWLEDGMENTS

This book has its roots in the vision of four women whose trust gave me the courage to believe I could accomplish more than I had ever dreamed: Sister Miriam P. Cooney, C.S.C., PhD, Sister Maria Concepta McDermott, C.S.C., PhD, who died soon after this research began, Becky Drury, PhD, Saint Mary's College and Linda Lucas, PhD, the University of Notre Dame. They called me out of the depths of my sabbatical and presented me with the challenge of writing a book on the role of women in today's church. I am indebted to each of them for their continued interest and support throughout these past three years. They are a superb example of what can happen when women reach out to help other women.

This was specifically true of Becky Drury my "co-author" whose proficiency at fund raising, creative initiative and constant stimulation helped us both to realize what wonderful things sisters and other lay women can create together! Becky epitomized, by her around the clock encouragement and support, what it means to be there for another. My gratitude to her is immeasurable.

I am also indebted to my religious congregation, the Sisters of the Holy Cross, who gave me the opportunity to do this research. I am particularly grateful to the sisters in each country who assisted me in numerous ways, and to the sisters with whom I live, whose interest, support and help were a source of strength to me.

This study of women on four continents was fittingly housed at the Kellogg Institute for International Studies at the University of Notre Dame. I am especially grateful to Father Ernest Bartell, C.S.C., PhD, Executive Director, who along with the members of the Academic Committee of the Kellogg Institute took a chance on an unknown researcher in appointing me Guest Scholar.

Two others from the University of Notre Dame were outstanding contributors to the successful completion of this research: Dr. Rodney F. Ganey, Director, Social Science Training and

Research Data Center, and Dorothy East, Special Projects Coordinator. Dorothy was responsible for the tabulation of thousands of pages of data from Bangladesh, Brazil, Uganda and the United States (see Appendix A). Dr. Ganey's analysis, which appears in Appendix B, presents a succinct summary of the key concepts of the research.

From the beginning there were men and women who embraced my vision and supported me by their financial contributions, thereby making it possible for this work to come to successful completion. Among them I particularly want to thank Mary and Thomas A. Demetrio, Bernard J. Hughes.

I owe a special debt of gratitude to my readers: Sister Anna Clare O'Connor, C.S.C., Sister Joan Chittister, O.S.B., Anne Klimek, Becky Drury, JoAnn MacKenzie, Clyde I. Hause and David Schlaver, C.S.C., whose critique of the various chapters kept me constantly aware of those for whom this book was written. Thanks also to Sister Regina Coll, C.S.J., who edited the entire manuscript not only with her pen but also with her scissors.

I am particularly grateful to two gifted women. The first, Miriam Therese Winter, S.C.M.M., permitted the use of her psalms about women, which were a great inspiration to me and provide signposts throughout the book as challenges for the reader. The second, Birdie McElroy, graphic artist, portrayed the women in a manner that imprints them indelibly in our minds and hearts.

There are innumerable others among the laity and clergy, both men and women, who supported and encouraged me along the way. They have my heartfelt gratitude. However, my deepest thanks goes to the unnamed women in each of the four countries who cared enough about Jesus' message of equality for women to answer the questionnaire and to be interviewed. They are the flesh and blood, the heart and soul of this book. It was my privilege to be a part of their lives, if only for a short time. The church is blessed by their presence. I join my voice with theirs in proclaiming, "We are God's chosen people, we are a cherished gender, we are a royal priesthood! May women everywhere continue to rise up and claim their future!"

FOREWORD

It is somewhat of a truism that the center of gravity of the church in the next century will move from Europe and North America to what we know as the Third World. The church will be younger and poorer. It will also be influenced by women who are assuming positions of leadership in base communities and parishes. This cross cultural study by Sister Francis B. O'Connor, C.S.C., provides insight into what women in Third World countries as well as the United States expect of their church and what they are eager to share. It may come as a surprise to some in the First World that women from such different and varied backgrounds have such similar desires and dreams. This is especially so for those who may have believed that the women's movement is an American middle-class phenomenon. From the villages of Bangladesh and Uganda, to the *favelas* of Brazil, to the cities of the United States the message is the same, "We are God-gifted women who wish to share our gifts with the church."

While the message may be the same, African and Latino feminist theologians have challenged their Caucasian sisters to be more careful in speaking of women's experience when what is meant is the middle-class, educated, white women's experience. *Like Bread, Their Voices Rise!* makes an important contribution in adding the voices and experiences of women who are not usually heard to the conversation. It will enable a more nuanced theology to be developed.

What follows is a fine example of how theology is developing today. God is revealed in the lives of the people; reflection on that revelation is the stuff of theology. Without negating the contributions of scholars and theologians at work in universities, libraries and monasteries, we have come to realize that theology also develops in the life of the community. The work of scholars is challenged and enriched by the experience of the Christian community. Without it, theology is dead.

Great as I believe the contribution of this book will be to the ongoing discussion of the role of women in the church, I am

11

convinced that it is secondary to what happened to the women who participated in the discussions and interviews.

The poet Adrienne Rich challenges women "to unlearn not to speak." She dares them to reclaim their voices silenced by the customs and mores of their societies and their church. But unlearning is more difficult than learning. It requires a rejection of what had previously been accepted as true and appropriate. It requires a kind of conversion, a turning away from behavior that had been accepted as right and proper. It requires practice for it is never easy to break a habit. More, it requires courage—courage to abandon one image of the self and to begin to acquire another, courage to set one's thoughts before the community, courage to critique the status quo, courage to own one's voice, and finally courage to begin to change. Despite the difficulty unlearning occurs and new knowledge replaces the old. And things are never quite the same.

Women unlearning not to speak is, in my opinion, one of the greatest effects of the work of Sister Francis. While the research that she shares with the global church is invaluable, what happened to the women and to her in the process far outweighs that contribution. The process was indeed the message. Women who had not been asked before to express their ideas and concerns about the church found themselves at first hesitant and mute. But in the security of the atmosphere created by Francis and her sisters, they were soon able to articulate their thoughts and beliefs and have them affirmed.

Her questions and her conversations were crafted in such a way as to foster theological reflection. This is evident especially in the responses of the women in the second interview at each site. It is obvious that the women thought about what had been asked in the first meeting. Not only did they think about it, but they formed strong opinions which they were willing to defend.

Francis was sensitive to the possibility that the women might have felt a sense of insecurity and timidity. She therefore interviewed them in small groups in settings with which they were familiar. Under the shade of banana and mango trees, in parlors and courtyards where they often talked with their friends, the women were welcomed and made to feel comfortable. Conducting the interviews in a communal setting rather than individually, as is typical of so many surveys, not only provided support and challenge for the women, but also eliminated a sense of being tested or judged. Conversation flowed freely and ideas bounced off one another. Watching the videos of the interviews one is struck by the sense of relatedness and connectedness among the participants. The whole process modelled women's way of learning and thinking.

A word needs to be said about the work of the Sisters of the Holy Cross. Many of the women who were interviewed had been influenced by the sisters. The sisters have ministered with them, bringing them to a fuller realization of their dignity and of the good news preached by Jesus to women and men alike. The success of their work is witnessed by the ability of the women to express their own views, rather than echoing what sister said. The sisters gave of their gifts, but more importantly they enabled the women to reveal their own gifts to one another.

The women surveyed are not the only ones who were given voice by the experience. Sister Francis herself has found a new voice with which to speak. Her lectures and writings have taken on a fresh passion that energizes her audience. To hear her is to hear the voice of one speaking with the voices of the women she came to know in the past two years. She herself has unlearned not to speak.

Regina Coll, C.S.J.

INTRODUCTION

Until woman assumes her rightful place in Christian ministry, Christ has only one hand with which to heal, to strengthen, to touch, and to console.[1]

"It is difficult to sit down when you wear pants made of iron." This African proverb speaks directly to the purpose of this book. A few among the Catholic hierarchy in the United States have proven by their willingness to dialogue and listen to women that their pants are not made of iron. But what are these among so many? Until the institutional church calls all of its bishops to sit down in open dialogue with women around the world, we will continue to be given only the crumbs that fall from the clerical table.

As a Catholic sister who is acutely aware of Jesus' message of equality and justice for all, the exclusion and oppression of women in the church is an issue of great concern to me. Along with so many other laity and clergy alike, I cannot wait for the institutional church to decide to act. Like many Catholic women I find myself teetering on the margins of the church, belonging and yet not feeling totally included, torn by loyalty and love for the church and the knowledge that it is much less than what Jesus meant it to be.

My own background as a missioner for twenty years in Bangladesh, and my five-year role as Regional Superior of my congregation's missioners on four continents made me intensely aware of women's shadowy place in their local church. When I became Superior General of my congregation and interacted with the hierarchy in an official capacity, my awareness of women's reality in a patriarchal church became acute. This experience provided me with a vision of the world church that speaks exclusively to men, about men, and for the advancement of men.

In addition to being grounded in the international life of the Sisters of the Holy Cross, I have the further privilege of being part of the Kellogg Institute for International Studies at the University of Notre Dame. For three years I have had the opportunity to interact with eminent scholars from all parts of the world as they shared the results of their academic research. In this position I have also had access to the excellent resources of the university's Social Science Research Laboratory.

In refutation of Rome's assumption that women's desire for full participation in the church is only a North American "problem," this book reveals the striking similarities between the experiences and unfulfilled hopes of women on the four continents of Asia, Africa, South America and North America. Their responses to the questionnaires along with personal interviews validate the fact that women around the world have a passionate yearning for inclusion and a determination to come out of the shadows.

In an attempt to move across cultural and institutional barriers to find a common ground, I collected data from women in Bangladesh, Brazil, Uganda and the United States. The focus was on determining how women are awakening to their reality in the church, what they are doing to challenge the church to live the message of the gospel, and what they claim for themselves as equal members in the church. During each of the first two years devoted to this research, I spent from one to three months in each country gathering data.

I chose these three developing countries not only because they represent a spectrum of Catholic population ranging from 89% in Brazil, 50% in Uganda to .2% in Bangladesh, but also because Holy Cross sisters have been present there for decades. Without the assistance of these sisters who gathered the women, provided hospitality, offered experiential knowledge of the country, transportation, and translation, this book would never have been possible.

In addition, the theology of church in each of the three countries ranges from the liberation approach of Brazil to the traditional and ultra-traditional theology of Bangladesh and Uganda. The book compares the responses of women from diverse cultures living in distinctly different Catholic milieus to those of women in the United States whose church experiences are as dissimilar as their ethnic and racial backgrounds.

In my first meeting with the women in each of the developing countries, their reactions to the questionnaire ranged from skepticism and suspicion to interest and excitement. The universal comment was, "No one has ever asked us what we think about the church before!"

When I returned the following year for individual and group interviews, the women were ready and waiting to tell their stories. I was greeted repeatedly with, "You said you would come back, and you did!" I sat with women in tiny rooms in *favelas* (open-air slums) both on the periphery and in the interior of Brazil. We also met in buildings constructed by the members of base communities. Ugandan women gathered in church buildings or on the grass at the edge of the jungle, some walking from five to ten miles to join the group. In Bangladesh we met in crowded villages and congested city homes. We sat together, mothers and children, old and young, on the ground in front of the bamboo and mud school buildings. In every instance the women testified to their rising awareness of the oppression they experience in the church. The planned thirty-minute interviews extended in many cases beyond two hours.

The data comprises samples in each of the three developing countries which are selective but typical of Catholic women identified by sisters and other lay pastoral ministers. The U.S. data was generated from three different subsamples. These include: a random sample from the Women's Ordination Conference, representing women who have been in the forefront of the struggle for equality in the church; a sample of selected but typical parish women identified by pastoral ministers both lay and religious; and Catholic women identified through a Gallup poll.

Women in the United States, whether on the east or west coast, in the southwest or midwest, were enthusiastic over the opportunity to be a part of this study. Typical of their attitude was the response of a Texas woman: "We are helping to write this book, that's certainly a way of getting the message out."

This book presents an in-depth exploration of the questions central to the life of Catholic women as they struggle to remain within the institutional church. It offers, in the words of one Catholic woman,

> . . . a rethinking of the questions lest once again the stories be told from one point of view, histories be constructed that exclude different or dissonant voices, "reality" be

defined by white, middle-class male experience, and symbol systems be controlled by the cleric.[2]

The three parts of this book narrate: 1) the responses of women in each of the four countries to a written questionnaire addressing their beliefs, attitudes and experiences as members of the church (the questions served to awaken many to an acute sense of their exclusion from the church); 2) interviews with women in each country eager to challenge the church's patriarchal stance against them; 3) a chorus of the voices of women in all four countries, who on the basis of scripture and theology claim their rightful place in the church as equal and full partners in the mystery of redemption.

The tension between the evidence of Jesus' treatment of women and how women experience the institutional church's treatment of them clearly reveals the necessity for dialogue, reconciliation and affirmative action. Women's voices make it impossible for the bishops of the world even to consider accepting a stalemate on the place of women in a church that preaches all are created equal.

The crumbs that fall from the clerical table no longer suffice to mitigate the hunger of these women. The bakers of bread are claiming their baptismal right to break open both the loaf and the word, in fulfillment of the gospel message of Jesus for them.

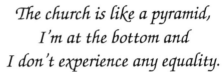

*The church is like a pyramid,
I'm at the bottom and
I don't experience any equality.*

—a Bangladeshi woman

Part 1

WOMEN
AWAKENING
TO THEIR REALITY
IN THE CHURCH

1

WOMEN, WHY DO WE WEEP?

U.S. women speak

For graces we have forfeited,
for capabilities untested,
for affirmation denied,
for deaths without resurrection,
for pain with no justification,
for hungers unsatisfied,
we weep.[1]

All the world over women weep! The reasons are many, and not the least painful is their exclusion from full participation in their church. Women's role in the Catholic Church has always been a subject of controversy. Martha and Mary, at the time of Jesus' visit to them in Bethany over two thousand years ago, exemplify the strain that has existed over the centuries among women. Martha chose the woman's traditional role. She welcomed Jesus into her home, but became distracted with much serving. Mary, however, preferred to sit at Jesus' feet and listen to his teaching, which in that culture identified her as a disciple of Jesus. Martha was upset and felt that Mary was out of place, so she complained to Jesus. His reply, "Let her alone," along with his refusal to force Mary into the stereotypical role of the women of his culture may have been his way of trying to help Martha understand there is more to life than being "busy." His response also indicated that he treated Mary as a person, and allowed her to set her own priorities. Jesus applauded her saying, "Mary has chosen the better part and it is not to be taken from her."[2]

A similar tension exists among Catholic women in the church in the United States today. Many want to maintain their traditional role and feel others should do the same. Like Martha, they get upset and complain when they see or hear of women who refuse to remain bound by tradition. These women, like Mary who chose the "better part," strive to set their own priorities; but unlike her they find that it has indeed *been taken away from them*! Taken away not by Jesus who maintained it would not, but rather by the very church founded on the teachings of Jesus. The patriarchal church, with all of its paternalistic dominance throughout the centuries, has successfully reversed Jesus' positive attitude toward women. It has forced women into a stereotypical role and deprived them of the freedom of setting their own priorities. It has made a mockery of the baptismal formula of the early church:

> There does not exist among you
> Jew or Greek, slave or free, male or female.
> All are one in Christ Jesus (Gal 3:27-28).

"This text is best understood as a communal Christian self-definition, an affirmation that within the Christian community no structures of domination can be tolerated."[3] Yet of all the types of domination, is there one deeper or more pervasive than the patriarchal oppression of women? It is no wonder that women weep!

In questioning nearly five hundred women in the United States regarding their role and participation in the Catholic Church, a multiplicity of responses indicated there are varieties of Marthas and Marys among us:

> women who want to maintain their traditional role in the church and want others to do the same;

> women who are content with the status quo, but don't object to others who are striving to achieve more in the church;

> women who strongly oppose the inequality born of the patriarchal system and work for full participation for women in the church;

women who see the injustices, but feel they don't have the time or energy to do anything about them;

Lastly, and most lamentable of all:

women who, because they can no longer endure the injustice, have turned to other churches or sources for spiritual nourishment that they cannot find in the Catholic Church.

There are certainly variations in all of these groups, but for the most part the responses fall into two categories: those who are content for whatever reason, and those who have a holy discontent and desire the "better part"—women's equality in the church.

Scripture does not tell us how Martha and Mary settled their differences. However, we can assume that following Jesus' example, they were able to accept and respect one another's unique call to discipleship and work together to build the kingdom. Women and men today, no matter what their education, age or ethnic background, must do the same.

The Catholic Church in the United States

Women comprise 57% (33.1 million) of the 58 million people in the United States who claim to be Catholic, while 63% of regular Mass attendees are women.[4] This "female face" of the church is repeated in women's participation in parish activities. The list is exhaustive. Women serve in altar preparation; as teachers and sponsors of the catechumenate; and as leaders of Bible and discussion groups, recreational and youth programs, parish renewal and prayer groups, as well as programs designed to help the poor and visit the sick and grieving. While women share equally with men as lectors, over 60% of eucharistic ministers are women. This closely parallels the number of women who attend Mass.[5] Women have indeed invaded the circles of parish leadership, but they do not have the influence nor are they as likely as men to be found in the "inner circles."[6]

The Catholic women who participated in this survey were contacted in three different ways: a Gallup sample, a sampling of women who belong to the Women's Ordination Conference

(W.O.C.), and women from selected parishes in heavily Catholic areas of the country. All three samples included Hispanic, Afro-American and Anglo-American women, as well as a range of age, education, professions and economic status.

The Northeastern section of the country has the heaviest concentration of Catholics. Fifty-nine percent are in New England, the Middle Atlantic, or East North Central states. Each decade, however, sees a continual growth of the proportion of Catholics shifting to the South and West.[7] Approximately two-thirds tend to live in urban and suburban areas, while over a third are in smaller city, town and rural parishes. The American Catholic population is becoming more international and multicultural as the number of Central and South American as well as Asian immigrants increases.

Just as there is no such thing as a typical Catholic parish in the United States, neither is there a typical Catholic woman. What is evident, however, is that there is indeed a typical critical issue for a great number of Catholic women in the United States today. That issue is exclusion, the restriction of women from full participation in decision-making, leadership positions and sacramental ministry in the church. Women from all over the United States expressed deep feelings about this issue:

> I believe the refreshing breath of women is being smothered in this church. Their issues are trivialized and will remain so until the patriarchal attitude of the church is deflated and new paradigms emerge (Flemington, NJ).

> I feel that I am treated as a slave, subservient to men, prevented from participating fully because of my sex (Pittsburgh, PA).

> As long as one group of people has power by virtue of gender over another group, *institutional apartheid* exists. That's what we see in our church today (San Jose, CA).

> Women (and lay people in general) have been thrown a few crumbs by the hierarchy (Dallas, TX).

These comments and those of many other women who suffer from the injustices of a patriarchal church are eloquently reinforced by Maria Riley, O.P. in her book, *In God's Image:*

> The critical issue is the patriarchal structure of the institutional church. The leadership at every level is male. Ordination is where patriarchy is most evident, although ordination is not the central question for most women. Exclusion is. Women are excluded from effective power in helping to shape the church's mission, its teaching, its law, its liturgy. After the decisions are made, women are granted their "appropriate" role. Women do not even have a voice in defining what is appropriate for them.[8]

Women who speak to the pain of patriarchy are not just trying to gain power or to enhance themselves. The issue is one of justice in the church, and they recognize that the effectiveness of the church's teaching on justice in our world depends upon the example it gives by its own internal reforms in this area. Pope John XXIII, in his 1963 encyclical *Pacem in Terris*, described the emergence of women into public life as one of the distinguishing characteristics of our age. He saw it as a distinctive sign of the times, one which we must carefully heed if we are to preach the gospel authentically in this century.

How can the church, the prophetic voice of God, continue to lag behind the secular world in recognizing this significant sign of the times? Women's gifts and talents have been left to lie fallow in the church these two thousand years. There is still time to cultivate and harvest them as women offer their service to the church today in ever increasing numbers. The twentieth century is coming to a close and yet the gospel has not been heard by literally millions of people in our world. If John XXIII had lived, he would surely have echoed St. Paul's words, "Now is the acceptable time" (2 Cor 6:2). Now is the time to put patriarchy behind us! Now is the time for women and men to work together as equals preaching the mission of Jesus.

The Catholic women surveyed reflect the attitudes of the U.S. women in general who are in search of equality. Over 96% of the respondents indicated they believe Jesus Christ wills men and women to be treated as equals. Eighty-nine percent, regardless of marital status, believe that women are equal to men; significantly more urban women hold this belief. Almost 91% want to be treated as equals; more highly educated women were strongest in this opinion. When asked whether they experience equal treatment by men, the responses ranged from a woeful 22% who said yes, to 64% who said sometimes.

Most frequently sighted as hindrances to their efforts to be treated equally were family tradition, male dominance, social mores, unequal compensation and other women. Clearly we have our Marthas and Marys in society as well as in the church.

The conflicting opinions of Catholic women regarding social equality are certainly mirrored in their struggle for full participation in the church. The belief that Jesus Christ wants women and men to be treated as equals in the church was affirmed by more than 81% of all respondents. In addition, women of all three samples were strong in their opinion regarding the church's treatment of them. Over 96% of W.O.C., 77.6% of parish and 67.7% of Gallup respondents felt that the mission of Jesus for women is not being carried out by the church today (Appendix C).

In each of the three samples, 100% of the sisters responding affirmed that the message of Jesus regarding women is not being lived in the church today. Single, married and divorced women strongly concurred. In general, older women did not perceive the church living the message of Jesus in regard to women. These women over forty have experienced the church both before and after Vatican II. Their responses indicate that they believe the church has not fulfilled the true meaning of Jesus' message for women.

The obstacles most frequently indicated which prevent women from ministering more effectively in the church today are clericalism, exclusive language, paternalism, male chauvinism, the attitudes of bishops, the attitude of Rome, and racism. Paternalism and the attitude of Rome toward women were cited most often.

If, as Maria Riley and so many of the women interviewed have said, exclusion is the critical issue for women in the church today, what does inclusion or full participation mean to these women? The questionnaire offered five definitions of full participation and the respondents had the opportunity to affirm or negate each.

Full participation for women

Equal decision-making power with men was affirmed as integral to full participation by 94% of the Gallup sample, 93% of the parish sample and 100% of the W.O.C. sample. Overall, the more highly educated women were significantly stronger in their response.

Ninety-two percent of Gallup, 89% of parish women and 100% of W.O.C. see equal leadership roles as full participation. Thirdly, a minimum of 94% in all three groups see equal ministerial roles, such as eucharistic ministers and lectors, as essential to the definition.

The fourth issue regarding participation concerned equal opportunity to preach the homily. This is seen by over 75% of Gallup, 82% of parish women and 99% of W.O.C. to be a significant part of full participation. These women were more likely to be highly educated, located in urban settings with modest incomes. Marital status did not affect their response.

Equal access to ordination was the fifth definition of full participation. This exemplifies inclusion for 53% of Gallup women, 65% of parish women and 98% of W.O.C. for an average of 72%. These were predominantly sisters, widows and single women, living in urban areas, highly educated and with moderate to low incomes. How frequently women attended the eucharistic celebration had no significant affect on their responses. It could be assumed that married women's responses were lower because they were influenced by the church's mandatory celibacy law for priesthood. (See Appendix C.)

As would be expected, women belonging to W.O.C. are highly desirous of inclusion in all the categories. However, the other women while exhibiting a more moderate response toward ordination are only slightly less eager for decision-making roles, leadership positions, and preaching the word.

Women crying out for inclusion are offering the church the opportunity to become whole. For centuries the church has been and is walking on one leg, seeing with one eye, hearing with one ear, speaking from half a heart and functioning with half the intellectual resources available to it.[9] Women's inclusion would provide woman-power to a man-powered church, the combination of which would symbolize a wholeness not yet experienced by the People of God.

The hopes of these women for inclusion, that is, to share their gifts, intelligence, insights, as well as to preach the gospel in our time are continually being denied. They look to the church for justice, and the response to them from John Paul II is, "... to imitate those aspects of servanthood, lowliness and humility which are emphasized in the life of Mary."[10]

Marcello Azevedo, S.J., gives a poignant assessment of the church's treatment of women:

> The church has multiple statements recognizing equality. In the Second Vatican Council the gospel inspiration of this equality was clearly and forcefully underscored. Nevertheless, the church has not made concrete and real as yet what it believes and proclaims. In today's world, the church remains one of the last bastions of radical anti-feminism in terms of practice, while paradoxically it is one of the most active defenders of the liberation and promotion of women on the level of principles.[11]

And still we are asked, "Women, why do you weep?"

The W.O.C. women surveyed are representative of the over 4,000 members who keenly feel the church's practice of anti-feminism, and are currently struggling to advance the cause of equality for all women in the church. Between 70% to 95% of W.O.C. women participate in activities such as writing letters, signing petitions, engaging in women's liturgies, and assisting with financial support. Women in the other samples were far less involved in these activities, with current participation ranging from 2.4% to 37.1%. Approximately 48% of the W.O.C. women join marches and boycotts, while nearly 10% of parish women and only 2.4% of Gallup respondents report involvement in these activities. Sixty percent of W.O.C. are withholding financial support from the church in contrast to about 12% of the other two groups.

When asked what they would be willing to do to obtain inclusion in the church, there was a significant increase in the response from all three sample groups, particularly the women in the Gallup and parish samples. In the areas of signing petitions, writing letters and engaging in women's liturgies, their willingness rose as high as 44%. The number willing to withhold financial support from the church was over 62%. This increase indicates that once women's awareness is raised to the injustices in the church they respond with energy and zeal. If this is the case, we might ask why women are so often their own worst enemies?

> Women have for millennia participated in the process of their own subordination because they have been psychologically shaped so as to internalize the idea of their own inferiority. The unawareness of their own history of struggle and achievement has been one of the major means of keeping women subordinate.[12]

Until women's awareness and conviction of their own worth becomes more of a norm, they will continue to allow themselves to be oppressed by the patriarchal behavior of both men and women. "In Christ we are called to relate to the fullness of humanity, not the perfection of masculinity."[13] This is a difficult lesson to learn after so many centuries of conditioning, but as women's perception of themselves is more clearly focused, they will see the power and potential the fullness of their humanity can bring to a church whose vision of women is still so hopelessly blurred.

Some women do see themselves and their potential very clearly. When asked whether their hopes regarding the inclusion of women as ministers in their Sunday liturgy were fulfilled, 35% of Gallup, 43% of parish and 76% of W.O.C. respondents said no they were not. In this study there is a significant inverse relationship between education and the degree of satisfaction with one's participation in the church. Those respondents who expressed a sense of unfulfillment were highly educated and predominantly sisters. Their words express the pain of their rejection:

> I feel called strongly to minister. I believe God loves me no less because I am a woman.

> The Holy Spirit is calling women to do many things, the hierarchy is denying women the chance to fulfill that call.

Women are viewed only as labor, never as management. We are the least valued of the flock. When there were not enough Catholic males to serve on the altar, the pastor invited "non-Catholic" males rather than Catholic females. What message are we given?

I feel like all I am asked or allowed to do in the Catholic Church is contribute money and "slave labor."

I'm angry, hopeless, wondering if it's worth bothering with. I feel so hurt, and attending church is so painful that I have stopped going.

I believe the church has sacrificed a great deal of creative energy by denying women's gifts. We are all the poorer for it. Women have been denied the right to celebrate their baptismal gifts.

The hopes of these women are not unlike the hopes and the pain of a woman over a century ago who, in spite of the church's rejection of her gifts, risked everything to respond to God's call to ministry on her own. She took responsibility for her own life, broke through the barriers imposed by her faith, culture, society and tradition, and with unprecedented results! Florence Nightingale expresses her anguish:

I would give her (the church) my head, my hand, my heart. She would not have them. She told me to go back and crochet in my mother's drawing room. "You may go to Sunday school if you like," she said. But she gave me neither work to do for her nor education to do it.[14]

Is it any wonder that women weep for all their unrealized potential?

Because the church has repeatedly refused to accept their gifts of ministry, many women today have no way of exercising them within the church. Some have gone elsewhere, choosing to minister in other churches thereby depriving not only Catholic men but other women as well of their service. Others continue to hope that the hierarchy will soon realize that like Jesus, the Spirit calls women as well as men to the "better part." Still others are breaking through the barriers imposed by their faith, culture, society and tradition by being assertive, bold and courageous when they continue to challenge the church to fulfill the mission of Jesus in their regard.

We share a deep desire to fully participate in the mission of Jesus. We are all victims of a system and circumstances over which we have little control. We have a responsibility to help the church reflect the reign of God more faithfully in the here and now.

Administering the sacraments of the sick, baptism and reconciliation, along with preaching the word of God are the ministries women in all three sample groups feel most called to perform. These sacraments require a special presence at times of birth and death as well as times of sickness of both soul and body. The need to respond to such moments in the lives of the People of God is equally as strong as the need to break open the word of God and share it from a woman's point of view. Sisters and women over forty were most desirous of these ministries. Their training and/or life experiences have prepared them to respond to these ministerial needs.

Presiding at the eucharist consistently ranked fourth in all groups, indicating that these women view priesthood within a broad ministerial context. It is from women such as these that a new vision of priesthood is evolving, a priesthood that will enable women and men truly to be partners in the mystery of redemption.

The question of ordination

Women of faith, evoking faith in each other, will build a church open to receiving the creative ministry of all its members. This support is evident in the response to the questions relating to ordination. Even among the W.O.C. members, many more women are in favor of ordination for other women than desire it for themselves. The responses indicate over 96% W.O.C., 65% parish and 46% Gallup desire ordination for other women. At the same time, 39% W.O.C., 16% parish and only 3% Gallup desire it for themselves (see Appendix C).

In general, sisters, single, divorced and highly educated women are significantly supportive of women's ordination. Over

60% of all women attending Mass either regularly or irregularly support the ordination of women. These figures and the personal responses demonstrate the Marthas supporting the Marys in their choices of the "better part":

> I don't necessarily want to participate in all things but I feel others should have the right to do so.

> As a woman, I am concerned about other women's struggles for what "should be."

> We struggle to obtain our place in the church and the Lord's ministries as Jesus so intended.

> Our struggles are identical. We have a common bond and affection, and a great desire to see Jesus' teachings put into practice.

> We are all very sad that we are not offered full membership. Why bother to baptize women?

Women's support for women, coupled with a strong desire to identify with and learn more about other women of the world is described by Dolores L. Greeley, R.S.M.:

> It is a fact that women, as members of the global community, whether from developed or developing nations, no longer accept the discrimination and inequalities they have endured for ages. They are networking to bring about change. Women want to walk together in solidarity on the journey toward liberation and a new society.[15]

Another area in which the women surveyed were strongly united was in their agreement that the equality of men and women is an integral part of the mission of Jesus. If women could minister in the church equally with men, the church would be a great deal closer to fulfilling that mission:

> The question is really more one of inclusion, until women minister equally with men in the church, there will be no true inclusion of all believers, there will be no true community in the tradition of Jesus.

I think if we ever get to the point where women are treated as equal, we will have a more gentle, patient, loving church. A church that will better reflect the balance between male/female that Jesus himself reflected.

Jesus came to liberate all people and to call them to new possibilities and new discipleship. Keeping women from this is keeping Jesus' mission from true fulfillment.

God's love would be more fully revealed; women's baptism would not be seen to be inferior; the sacraments would be given to more people; the gospel would be preached with greater authenticity.

These arguments indicate that the respondents have, according to Rosemary Ruether, ". . . an enormous and exhausting task on their hands, viz. the radical transformation of the church."[16] If in fact, as the women surveyed so strongly indicate, God did not ordain women to have secondary and subordinate positions in the church, then the church's patriarchal structure is a distortion of the gospel and ". . . it makes sense for those who can endure the pain to remain and to struggle until the church becomes the 'discipleship of equals' which Jesus initiated."[17] Women's role today is to challenge the church to live the true message of the gospel. Many women have already begun to issue this challenge:

The church has placed a "glass ceiling" on the role of women in the church. It is the male hierarchy that says no to women, not God.

I think the church is patriarchal and sexist. Women are active in the church and do ministry but we are ignored in church language, sacraments and positions of power. I am angry about this and think it sinful. I want the church to be a leader in the women's movement because of the gospel message.

I feel the Catholic Church needs to wake up and join the modern world. It is time for men and women to be treated as equals. The church is cold and impersonal. I feel that if change doesn't come soon, membership will continue to fall.

How much longer will the church continue to turn a deaf ear to half of its membership?

Women should be allowed to choose priesthood just as men can choose. It is a matter of justice as well as common sense. I am not allowed to receive orders, I have no option, whether I am called or not. I believe this is really sinful and totally un-Christ-like.

For centuries women have filled the pews on Sunday, taught their children, volunteered endless hours for the church while men make the decisions, have key leadership roles, spend the money and keep women in their place.

This exclusion is illustrated very graphically by one woman who describes the emptiness and desolation of being treated as a second-class member of the church, "I sit in the pews keeping the seat warm while my soul is freezing to death." Most women speak of their strong desire to minister, but this woman depicts the reality of the death of the spirit in many whose souls cry out for nourishment.

Jesus clearly stated that the Marys of this world have the right to choose the "better part," to be equal disciples with men. Discussion of this God-given right is not even allowed in official circles of the church. The power that bishops and clerics reserve to themselves prohibiting women's response to God's call to priesthood is frightening indeed. They would profit by reflecting on the words of Gamaliel who gave sage advice to those who would prevent the early Christians from practicing their faith. "Leave these people alone. If what they teach and do is merely on their own, it will soon be overthrown. But if it is of God, you will not be able to stop them, lest you find yourselves fighting even against God" (Acts 5:38-39, *Today's English Version*).

Women in the church today, whether they are more comfortable in the role of Martha or Mary, have a great responsibility. If they embrace the challenge of calling the church to radical transformation, they themselves must support and sustain one another in the struggle that inevitably will come about. Until that embrace becomes a reality, many women will continue to weep.

Weep with us, for us, in us,
as we struggle through pain
toward a new tomorrow
when we will weep no more.[18]

2

WHO CARES ABOUT US?

Ugandan women ask

Happy are we when we can be ourselves
and be thoroughly accepted,
when our identity and personality
are appreciated and affirmed.[1]

Who are Ugandan women? What is their social, economic, political and religious status? Why do they cry out for recognition, acceptance and appreciation? Are they somehow unique or are they typical of other women in developing countries? The Honorable Miria Matembe, Commissioner, Ugandan Constitutional Commission, focused on some of these issues at a seminar in Jinja, Uganda in June, 1990. Her keynote address was entitled: "The Situation of Women in Uganda."

Women in Uganda, like their counterparts everywhere in the world, have been given secondary citizenry. This low status is established by customs and cultural practices and endorsed by some legislation. Both cultural attitude and lack of economic independence enhance women's inferior status: a woman is a property of her father when she is a young girl and becomes a property of her husband upon exchange of bride price. Being a property, she is not entitled to make decisions of her own and she owns nothing. The very reason for which she came into this world is to produce children and toil to maintain the children and the clan.[2]

Uganda and its people

Over nine million women endure this oppression in a country that was once termed "Africa's Garden of Eden." Set in the heart of Africa, Uganda is a land-locked country in the western rift valley. Its lush fertile soil provides food for approximately seventeen million people. The severe economic condition of the country is evidenced by the fact that government salaries have been below subsistence level for over ten years. No public servant, however frugal, could survive on this salary. This is true for most of the working population. Everyone is expected to have additional means of income such as a small business or shop. Teachers often have positions in two or three schools at the same time in order to earn a living. In spite of this, they can barely feed their children let alone clothe and educate them. Because of the low salaries, the official work day is only four or five hours to enable people to work two or three jobs.

Uganda is one of the least urbanized countries in Africa, and ranks eighth lowest in the world. Ninety-one percent of the population live in rural areas. Kampala, the capital and largest city numbers 500,000, while Jinja, the next largest city, has only 50,000 inhabitants. In other towns, one can easily walk from one end to another in thirty minutes. The population is young, approximately 50% are under fifteen years of age. Four main language groups, each including several subdivisions, along with regional, cultural and ethnic differences constitute the underlying causes of much of Uganda's recent strife.[3]

Ugandan women, like other women of Africa, are the backbone of the rural economy. They provide 80% of the agricultural labor with a workday varying from twelve to eighteen hours, and walk anywhere from one to five miles to haul firewood and fetch water. Women dig in the fields and produce the food the family eats while still bearing and caring for the children. Yet they cannot own or inherit land, are not encouraged to go to school and, in many instances, believe that wife-beating is an acceptable practice. Ugandan men own the land which the women work and sell the food which the women produce, thereby controlling the cash. Many men equate controlling money with work and do not describe what women do as work.

40

An African proverb says: "Better to have a husband that beats you than no husband at all." To offset belief in this proverb the Ugandan Women's Lawyers Association recently embarked on a campaign to convince women that wife-battering is not a sign of a man's love.[4] In spite of these efforts, many women have nowhere to go and cannot change their circumstances by escaping from violent and oppressive husbands. Education for women is still thought of as unnecessary by many people. Parents who send their girls to school often withdraw them after a few years. Nearly twice as many women, 60%, as men, 35%, are illiterate.

Ugandan men often go to the cities to search for jobs and leave the women alone in the villages. Since an estimated 50% of marriages in Uganda are polygamous, and among monogamous marriages faithfulness to one wife is not highly valued, many Catholic women are faced with a moral dilemma. Either they accept an unfaithful husband along with the possibility of contracting AIDS or reject him and face starvation for themselves and their children. The overall demographic impact of AIDS has not been sufficiently studied as yet. However, the increase in AIDS deaths of both women and men between the ages of twenty-five and forty may set the stage for a nation of orphans and elderly in the next generation. AIDS is a growing threat especially to women in Uganda.

> It is estimated that a half million women are HIV-positive. The World Health Organization estimates that the death rate of women in the child-bearing age bracket will increase by 30% in areas with infection by the mid-1990s due to AIDS.[5]

Who in government cares about these Ugandan women?

Until recently when the National Resistance Movement (NRM) government came into existence in 1986, the Ugandan government certainly did not care about its women. This present government, however, has begun supporting women in their struggles and has created a "Ministry of Women in Development" which serves as the focal point for the formation of strategies to address the concerns and needs of women. Each government committee, at every level, is mandated to have at least one female representative who is responsible for women's affairs. This is an initial step in the recognition of the equality of women. Notwithstanding, one woman on an all male council has little opportunity to sway the vote, especially when her presence and voice are reluctantly received. In addition, women frequently do not come to public gatherings which are predominantly male because they do not have proper clothes to wear or they are afraid to speak in front of men. They also know that their husbands do not like to see their wives taking part and often suspect the women of ulterior motives.

In order to give women more voice, as well as to create an atmosphere in which they can speak freely, a new proposal is being prepared to create a Women's Council from the grassroots to the highest levels of government. Women, however, will still have to deal with husbands who resent the time this effort might take away from their home or farm work.

The Prime Minister of Uganda, Dr. S.B.M. Kisekka, highlights other ways the government cares for women:

> The Government has also made it a premium concern to lift up the status of women and empower them to cope with the multiplicity of the roles they play in our society, not only through the Resistance Committee system but also by strengthening their contribution in all sectors of our community.[6]

Nonetheless the problem, says Magdalene Kyomukama, who works in the Planning Division of the Ministry of Women in Development, Culture and Youth, is to reach women in the rural areas of the country. The number of women in government positions is extremely limited, and travel is slow and difficult. The main channel of communication to women is the radio, but only 34% of all rural women have access to a radio. In addition, those who have money to buy a radio often cannot get batteries which are expensive or unavailable. The government has indeed made some efforts to care for women, but it is obvious that a great deal more must be expended before the ordinary Ugandan woman in the "bush" will even begin to feel the impact.

Who in Ugandan society cares about women?

In the national newspaper *The New Vision*, September 5, 1991, Miria Matembe points a finger at society when she says, "Ugandan society nurtures and cherishes customs and cultural practices which are oppressive to women." She quotes Mikhail Gorbachev:

> As a matter of fact what women give society and what they are capable of giving it depends in turn on the capacity of society to give women real rights and social protection and to provide them with the social dignity they deserve.

She continues with her observation that Ugandan society has not done what Gorbachev suggests. She insists there is an urgent need to amend the laws in order to give women the legal rights and protection that they deserve.

Many Ugandan women are strong in their desire for more rights in society while others are unaware of their oppression. Joan Kakwenzire, the only woman on the Uganda Human Rights Commission, elaborates this fact when she says:

> Some women in Uganda have embarked on a very long walk from a state of subjection and oppression to freedom, while others have not yet begun. Yet others do not even know that they are subjugated and oppressed and therefore they are content in what others regard as misery.[7]

A recent survey of Uganda women's needs, conducted through Makerere University in Kampala, describes what a voluntary non-government organization, formed by women in 1985 is doing:

> Action for Development was formed to stimulate the awareness of the nation to their potential rights, as well as to expand the involvement and visibility of women in Uganda's development. Its role is to:
>
> —conscientize women and men
> —educate women
> —initiate projects of benefit to women
> —organize research about women
> —give legal and political advice with emphasis on women.[8]

In spite of society's efforts thus far, Ugandan women experience grave injustices and openly express their pain over how they are treated:

> As a woman, there are so many things I cannot do; my father must accept a dowry despite the fact that I'm educated, I must submit to a man as my superior, I have no inheritance rights, and I cannot be ordained to religious ministry.

> I feel men's domination, suppression and low opinion of women. They still refuse a woman a chance for self-expression, and best positions everywhere are reserved for men.

> I would like to rise up and participate equally with men. Women need to be respected, to be given a chance to give their views, to be given privileges and proper learning as the men.

> Women are very oppressed because men think they know everything and are masters of everything. Hence, they always want women at their feet.

A woman working in the diocesan office feels that the most important contribution she can make is to raise women's awareness to their lack of liberty and freedom. At the same time she is convinced that change for women will come only when women themselves want to change, when they begin to understand what freedom means for them. "It will never be given them from men," she says, "because men have it too good!"

Who in the church cares about Ugandan women?

Unfortunately women are most often treated as children rather than adults by local clergy and hierarchy alike. In marriage disputes or when they are victims of their husband's drunken violence they are counseled to go home and "be a better wife," as if they were the guilty ones. Women's contributions to the church in parish life and all supportive roles are seen as crucial for the life of the church, but women are totally absent in decision-making arenas and in the planning levels. Like children, women are to be seen, but not heard.

Over two hundred women responded to my questionnaire regarding their role and participation in the Catholic Church. The overall recurring theme in their responses was: "I would like to be respected for who I am and the gifts I bring as a woman!" Ninety-six percent said that they believe Jesus wants his church to treat women and men as equals. Well over half of the women felt that the church is either not living the message of Jesus for women or there were times when it does not (see Appendix C).

Their desire for respect was expressed in different ways. One woman pointed out that even though she had reasonable suggestions at meetings, the ideas were not considered important because they were put forth by a woman. Others indicated that some priests do not invite women to meetings, nor do they consult them when preparing ceremonies. Priests merely assign them jobs. A large number, almost 65%, particularly young women and those from the city, hope for a greater participation in the Sunday liturgy than they are experiencing. These women tend to be among the educated and have knowledge of the teachings of Vatican II, while the older women for the most part do not. The younger women feel this exclusion deeply and spoke of their own pain as well as what they see as deprivation for the entire church because of this exclusion. The following quotations are typical of these women's responses:

> If women could minister equally with men, more people would be spreading the gospel and more would receive the Good News. More good decisions could be made by men and women and all would receive new ideas.

> Sometimes I wish I could be given the chance to teach and preach because there are times when I have ideas to share.

> I feel I want to be made a leader in the church so as to encourage Christians to be more committed.

> Men want to suppress the development of women. They are jealous when they see women progressing economically, socially and religiously. They don't want to see self-reliant women.

The church's lack of appreciation for women was evidenced when only 39% said they feel their pastor and bishop want full participation for women. Those who answered negatively supported their responses with comments like the following:

> The whole organization of church leadership and even informal settings point to the limitation or exclusion of women.

> When I asked the parish priest to critique my paper on "Religious Attitude Toward Politics," he told me I wasn't capable of managing this topic, it is for *men*! He suggested I write about the catechumenate which suits my knowledge.

> Our bishop thinks women are below the standard to teach in major seminaries, also that women's work is to do things that don't require intellect, e.g., washing priests' clothes and cooking for them.

This lack of appreciation of women is verified by Rodrigo Mejia, S.J.:

> If the attention to the dignity and active role of women in the church is important everywhere in the world it is indeed of special urgency in the African continent. . . . The faithful presence of women in liturgical celebrations, in movements and small Christian communities is far superior to that of men. All the same they are the outstanding absentees in the *lineamenta* document; they are mentioned just once together with millions of men, children and the aged. It is most unlikely that they will be given any particular consideration as victims of injustice and as agents of evangelization at this stage of preparation for the synod.[9]

The institutional church's care for Ugandan women does not fulfill their yearning for respect or their desire to participate. Women's responses to the meaning of full participation clarified their desire even more. Well over 90% indicated that equal opportunity for decision-making and leadership positions in the church is part of their understanding of full participation for women.

Over 75% affirmed that women should have the same opportunity as men to be eucharistic ministers and lectors as well as to give homilies. About a third expressed the belief that women's full participation should also include the opportunity to be a deaconess or a priest (see Appendix C).

These are the desires of mature women who carry the adult burden of feeding the nation, but are treated as children by their church. They are only permitted to fix flowers, clean the church, sing in the choir and do innumerable services behind the scenes, but are rarely, if ever, given the chance to share their wisdom or lived experience. Women or men who seek power and position in the church for their own benefit or who attempt to promote themselves are indeed to be feared, but the women questioned are motivated by the needs of their community, not their own profit or gain.

If I had more opportunity I could touch many lives, people are hungry for the word of God.

If women were given full participation, perhaps women's problems could also be discussed.

I would like to be able to give the sacraments since priests are not available.

The more opportunities I am given, the more the church will learn about women and the better person I would become.

I would like women catechists to be able to give holy communion.

Women's desire to minister is perceived by many clergy and hierarchy as suspect, and ulterior motives are imputed to them, while the same desire to minister expressed by men is perceived as a call from God! Did God not call all, women as well as men, into the vineyard? The harvest in Uganda is indeed great and the present laborers too few, yet the officials in the church refuse even to consider over half of its resources as potential ministers. Obviously it prefers the harvest to wither and die rather than allow women to minister.

The door to spiritual improvement is labeled, "Men only!" Women who desire the opportunity to study scripture and theology in order to help others understand their faith are denied entry. A sister who has dared to enter through that door has this to say:

> I believe women are asking the church to examine itself in relation to women, the attitudes of the clergy and hierarchy towards women, the ways women's cases are presented in our marriage tribunals . . . the exclusion of women from preaching to the whole people of God. Women continue to point out that the church's patriarchy is linked to an inadequate understanding and appreciation of the full potential and full vocation of women in the people of God. Because women are excluded at the heart of the church, the church itself lacks a fullness of human reflection, male and female, in the formation of its doctrinal, moral and pastoral life.[10]

How does the church reconcile this behavior with its own pronouncements on women? When the bishops gathered for the Synod on the Laity, they were confronted with the various forms of discrimination and marginalization to which women are subjected just because they are women. "The bishops affirmed the urgency to promote and defend the personal dignity of women and their equality with men."[11] The question must be asked, how many bishops are acting on this affirmation? African women heard the message of the bishops and

> . . . they are questioning the established order of things. In fact, the awakened awareness of the traditionally unquestioning women has scared some ecclesiastics into phasing out diocesan programs involving women's development and leadership. It has become uncomfortable for the clergy concerned to head a congregation of women who demand to know the wherefore, the what, and the how of their church's teachings and practices.[12]

Isn't it ironic that power and position for men are so blessed by the church while power and position for women, the so-called weaker sex, are so feared?

If perfect love casts out fear, perhaps it will not be until males . . . stop being afraid of . . . women and begin to love them as they love themselves that the church will be a true sign of Easter universalism.[13]

Do Ugandan women care about other women?

Ninety percent specified that they identify with other women of the world who struggle for equality in society, while 76% identify with women who struggle in the church. Some of the things they feel they have in common with these women are:

Courage!

We all want our abilities to be appreciated.

We want to work hand in hand to uplift women's rights.

We all desire full and equal participation with men.

We have many capabilities that are helpful for the upbringing of God's kingdom and society at large.

Their answers to questions inquiring about the ordination of women also indicate Ugandan women's care and affirmation of other women. In general, 49% are in favor of ordination for women, and 38% aspire to priesthood for themselves. Of these, significantly more are women who are poor, less educated and from the rural areas (see Appendix C). This is consistent with the fact that these women suffer from a lack of priestly ministry due to the shortage of priests. The educated and more affluent who live in cities have access to Mass and the sacraments on a regular basis. Several rural women spoke to the unnecessary waiting they are forced to do when the parish priest is late or fails to appear for Mass. "If we could celebrate it ourselves," they said, "our time would not be wasted." Almost 75% indicated that they would support other women who want to be trained for ordination even though they might not see themselves in that role.

Bernadette Kunambi sums up this affirmation when she says: "What all women need are opportunities, encouragement, awakening and acceptance in their rightful place in society (and in the church). Give women the tools and, with God's blessing, they will complete the job!"[14]

How does Jesus care for Ugandan women?

Ugandan women seek the acceptance and recognition denied them by their government, their society and even their church in the person of Jesus of Nazareth. Because they are among the poor and most marginalized, they can praise him with a certain sense of familiarity: "Yesu, (Jesus) who has received the poor and makes us honorable, our exceedingly wise friend, we depend on you as the tongue depends on the jaw."[15]

Not unlike the woman in the gospel who came out of the shadows to touch Jesus' garment and was cured of her blood disease, women of Africa are driven by a similar sense of hope. Ugandan women were born and many are still living in the shadows of history, where, says Rosemary Haughton, "women have lived since there was a history, for history was written by men."[16] They are also suffering from an incurable disease, that of being diminished, devalued and excluded by their male counterparts, both lay and cleric.

> In reaching out her hand, the gospel woman becomes the symbol of all the women who, conditioned and habituated to insignificance, still find in themselves a small flame of unexplainable hope that things may be different, and reach out towards what they recognize in some way as the fire which has lighted their flame.[17]

African women have that small flame of hope and reach out their hand to Jesus, the one who is sensitive to their misery and oppression and who in his own time sought to liberate and empower women.

> Jesus bears in his person the conditions of the weak and hence those of women. However, African women warn that it is vicarious suffering, freely undertaken, which is salvific, and not involuntary victimization. The passion of Christ was a voluntary result of his spirituality.[18]

Ugandan women freely suffer as they bear and care for their children, but more and more are becoming aware that in other areas of their lives they are involuntary victims of man-made injustices. At this time in history, with a growing sense of self-worth, they reach out to other women who are in solidarity with them and proclaim:

> God made me and I am good,
> because I am a woman.
> I share in God's own Motherhood,
> because I am a woman.
> The image of God is image of me,
> because I am a woman.
> God will give the victory,
> because I am a woman.
> God said, Daughter, don't be sad
> because you are a woman.
> And I said, I am very glad,
> because I am a woman![19]

3

DON'T SILENCE US!

Bangladeshi women's voices

Help us to speak wise words
when we challenge our traditions
and seek to offer alternatives
to the platitudes and the rules.[1]

Bangladesh is a country in which women are regarded as a burden from the day they are born. This fact was illustrated graphically in a recent article entitled, "Don't Silence Me" which appeared in Bangladesh. The author, Q.A. Tahmina, pointed out: "Even after millennia of human civilization, a woman is born in many parts of the world less than human. She, the tree of life, is born merely a girl child."[2]

Black and white pictures starkly depicting the life of the girl child of Bangladesh punctuate the story. The silent accusation in the scarred, malnourished face of a small child lures the reader to the helpless muteness in the eyes of a mother resting her hand on a sleeping baby girl. The mother's gesture indicates her desire to protect the child whose fate is forever entwined with her gender. Their faces are only a glimpse of the dismal and depressing reality of millions of Bangladeshi girls and women deprived of the basic necessities of life along with any voice in their society. Women are, in fact, mute.

Bangladesh, the country and society

To understand these women it is essential to also understand their country and their culture. Bangladesh is an Islamic state with a Hindu minority of about 10%. It is a country comparable in size to the state of Wisconsin. It has a population of over 110 million, less than .2% are Catholic. This small country, formerly a part of British India, became successively East Pakistan in 1947 and Bangladesh in 1971.

Bengalis and Tribals comprise the two major ethnic groups in Bangladesh. The Bengalis, who are a patriarchal society, are converts from Hinduism from the time of the Portuguese in the seventeenth century. The Tribals are recent converts from animism and are a matriarchal society. Tribals inhabit the northern and southeastern fringes of the country and are of Tibetan and Burmese extraction. The converts to Catholicism among them are rapidly outnumbering the Bengali Catholics.

Extreme poverty is combined with the highest density of population in the world. Women have a life expectancy of forty-seven years. The status of women is captured by Salma Khan:

> Although the vast majority of rural population are under-privileged, poor and illiterate, women are the poorest among the poor and have a much lower literacy rate than men: compared to a 30% rate of literate men only about 16% women are literate. In the traditional culture of Bangladesh, women bear the brunt of poverty and ignorance much more than their male counterparts. . . . The total life situation of a woman in Bangladesh is highly dependent on her status within the family as a daughter, wife or mother, and the material base of her family in the society.[3]

Credence is still given to the Bengali saying that "Educating your daughter is like watering another man's fields." Is it any wonder the literacy rate for women is so low? Catholic parents, however, are now beginning to change their attitude toward the value of educating their daughters, but some, unfortunately, for the wrong reasons. Girls are being permitted to attend school, particularly high school and college, not so much because they are seen as deserving an education, but rather because their education will enable them to contribute to the family income, manage the family home more intelligently, or obtain a more favorable marriage arrangement. Even though the literacy rate among Catholic girls is higher than the national average, it is still rare to find Catholic parents who feel that their daughters and sons should be equally educated.

It is very evident that male dominance is deeply entrenched and accepted among all religious groups in Bangladesh.[4] Since the Catholic population is such a small minority, they struggle to maintain their identity in a predominantly Muslim society. Muslim men have the power to seclude women through the imposition of *purdah* (the veil). There are no provisions within the Catholic community for men to impose such restraints on women.[5] Therefore, Catholic men are fearful of women's new freedom of movement which exposes them to the risk of leaving the church or to marrying outside their faith. Rather than being trapped in an undesirable marriage arrangement or because they are unable to find a suitable Catholic husband, many Catholic girls marry a Muslim and thereby relinquish their faith. Catholic men would like to have women more secluded than they are, but do not have the collective power to impose such restraints even though individual men try to do so.

Due to economic necessity following the 1971 war of independence, Catholic women, though small in number, stepped out of their village homes to act as leaders of cooperatives and managers and treasurers of cottage industry groups. These roles opened the doors for them to enter the marketplace and work world. In the cities they have moved in greater numbers into the professional roles of teachers, nurses, lawyers, doctors, government and business office workers. Along with these expanded roles has come a greater awareness of women's status both in society and in the Catholic Church.

As stated earlier, Bangladeshi women are socially conditioned from childhood to believe they are inferior to men, and are reared with a different set of values that enforce the ideas of male domination and female subordination.[6] Paradoxically, 70% said they believe that they as women are indeed equal to men. When over 80%, especially married women, said they wanted to be *treated as equals* with men, it was apparent that these women were aware of their plight and longed for equality, as do so many other women in the world. There was a significant difference in this regard between college educated women and those less educated;

the better educated said that men do not treat them as equals. Urban women and sisters were more inclined to concur. Rural women who, on the whole, are less educated and less aware of their oppressed situation, were more apt to say they are treated as equals by men.

Social customs, male dominance, family traditions and lack of equal education were most frequently mentioned as obstacles preventing women from achieving a sense of equality with men. In Bangladesh there are a few professional women's organizations dedicated to the cause of women. The presence of highly educated and emancipated women in these organizations enables them to play an important role as pressure groups and spokespersons for women's socio-economic rights. One of these groups, "Women for Women," (established in 1973) is the only women's organization focusing on research and public education for improving women's stand against oppression and exploitation.[7]

The fact that the total life situation of a woman in Bangladesh is highly dependent on her status within the family as daughter, wife or mother cannot be overstated. A woman in Bangladesh society has no name or identity of her own. Before she is married, a woman is not called by her own name, but is known as "Peter's daughter." After marriage, she is designated as "Andrew's wife," and when she has born a son, she is known as "Joseph's mother." Out of respect a wife never speaks her husband's first name. She, however, is nameless and seems to have no identity in and of herself. This lack of personal identity and anonymity is comforting to a few respondents, but painful to most.

As women's awareness regarding their role and position in society has increased, the desire to assume their own identity has also increased. This is reflected in the 81% who indicated they want to be called by their own name. A profile of the respondents in this category represents significantly more women who are married, Bengali, city-dwellers and educated. Conversely, 19% prefer to be known as someone else's daughter, wife or mother. As one Indian writer has so poignantly noted: "There are no women in this country; there are only men and their shadows."[8] This phenomenon is exemplified by Bangladeshi women when they cover their faces and heads in the presence of their husbands, walk two steps behind them in public, or stop speaking when they enter the room. These Bangladeshi women, like women in many cultures who are unable to seek their own identity, find their security being in the shadow of another.

When asked how they feel about their place in society and whether they would like to have more rights and privileges, almost three-fourths answered in the affirmative and gave the following reasons:

Women need freedom in society to defend themselves against the injustices of men.

A woman cannot go out alone, without a man!

I want to live like a human being.

I do not feel valued in society.

Married women, since they have less freedom of movement, were significantly more likely to want more rights and privileges than single women or sisters.

A little more than one-fourth indicated satisfaction with the status quo and are not desirous of more privileges. A few cited specific reasons which indicate that they are afraid to jeopardize what little security they have.

If we don't follow the present norms, we'll be deprived of what we have.

If we move beyond, we'll be seen as "bad women."

I am known in society as an honest, sincere and kind woman, that's enough!

In her book *Women, Tradition and Culture*, Malladi Subbamma, a prominent Indian woman journalist and writer, claims that 99% of Indian women do not *desire* social change. She refers to their self-designation as "kue ka meyndak" (frogs in a well)— people with intellectual and physical horizons limited to the tiny patch of sky directly above their heads.[9] How can any woman who is oblivious of the chains that bind her desire freedom?

Given these statistics, how is it that a small but vocal number of Christian educated women in India are actively working for change? Similarly, Catholic women in Bangladesh are becoming more aware of the bonds that are being broken by women in society all over the world, and are expressing a desire to jump out of the well!

The people of Bangladesh are poets, artists and dreamers. Their poetry and music were readily adapted at the time of the liturgical reforms following Vatican II. Among their hymns is a beautiful Bengali song that begins with the words, *"Shoono! shoono! shoono!*—Listen! listen! listen!" These words invited me to listen and to hear what Bangladeshi women today understand concerning their role in the Catholic Church. They believe that Jesus Christ wants women treated as equals with men. They describe the roles women want for themselves in the church.

Women's place in the church

The women of Bangladesh, both Bengalis and Tribals, in villages and cities, highly educated as well as uneducated, are all eager to speak. Single women, including sisters, housewives, teachers, nurses and professional women are anxious to be heard. Office and factory workers, students and house servants, all who have been kept in the shadows of society and the church are ready to speak because no one until now has ever asked them what they thought about their church. One young woman put it very succinctly when she said, "Our church doesn't give us a chance, it thinks women are inferior." Another chimed in, "No matter how wise or educated women may be, in our society, men are more important because they have leadership and priority."

How do these Bangladeshi women view their ministry in the church today? When asked if their hopes for the inclusion of women as ministers in the Sunday liturgy were fulfilled, 71% said yes. What does fulfillment mean to women who have only been permitted to perform such traditional roles as singing hymns, fixing flowers and preparing the altar?

These women have been conditioned by their culture and the church to believe they are "unclean" and therefore barred from the altar. They have been schooled to accept all the behind-the-scenes functions as their only roles and be satisfied with what might seem to western women as only "crumbs from the table." Some Bangladeshi women feel privileged to be permitted to perform these tasks and thus their minimal expectations are fulfilled. On the other hand, more than half of the women surveyed indicated they would like to be eucharistic ministers and nearly all would like to be lectors. Only lay men and sisters are presently permitted the privilege of being eucharistic ministers. Lay women are permitted to read in a few parishes on weekdays but rarely, if ever, on Sundays.

Women whose hopes for inclusion as ministers in the liturgy were not fulfilled gave the following reasons:

Our priest does everything himself, I have no opportunity to participate.

In our parish, we cannot read the scripture, distribute communion, or preach.

The hopes of these women, representing almost 30% of those surveyed, remain unfulfilled in spite of their awareness of what could be for them.

Of the women surveyed who acknowledged they had outgrown what they had formerly believed to be "their traditional place" in church ministry, married women were significantly more desirous of greater participation than sisters or single women. Sisters, because of their education and position, already have more opportunities to participate than lay women and appeared to be more satisfied with their degree of participation. The majority of single women who responded were professional women and, as a result, may have felt they did not have time for additional involvement in the church.

However, those who desire more involvement expressed their yearning in the following words:

Men and women should have the same privileges to facilitate the ministry.

I want to participate in planning and decision-making.

I feel chained and limited in my participation.

Thus, they hope for more and believe in Jesus' words to the woman in the gospel, "Woman, great is your faith, your request is granted." Women of Bangladesh are women of great faith. Will the church of Jesus not respond to them also?

When asked how they image God, nearly three-fourths indicated "Spirit." Only a very few saw God as female or male. Islam, with its distant God, its lack of images and its devotion to the "breath" of God, in this instance, leaves a positive imprint on the Catholic minority in the country. The spirit of Islam as well as the spirit of Hinduism and animism pervades the society in which this very small minority of Catholic women live, work and worship.

Full participation

Some revealing insights surfaced from the responses concerning the meaning of "full participation" for women in the church. Six different definitions were offered with the opportunity for respondents to mark each. Eighty-nine percent, largely urban women, agreed that equal decision-making power with men is a part of the definition. Eighty-five percent, more married than single women or sisters, felt that equal access to leadership positions is also essential. Since such a high percentage want to be lectors and eucharistic ministers, it was not surprising that 93% indicated equal ministerial positions such as these essential to "full participation."

When asked if "full participation" means equal opportunity to give homilies, almost 79% said it does. This was unexpected since women in Bangladesh society rarely speak in public and consistently defer to men because of cultural demands. However, when they come together in women's groups, they are very vocal indeed. Rural and married women, who are more subject to male domination, were stronger in their desire to give homilies than women from the city, single women or sisters. These latter have more opportunity to express themselves professionally and socially. Tribal women are leaders in a matriarchal society and are comfortable speaking both at home and in public. Therefore, their desire to give homilies is far stronger than that of the more oppressed Bengali women.

Is it because for the most part these women have been denied the right to speak other than in their homes or in women's groups, that they exhibit such a strong desire to speak out in their church today? Or is it that some women in Bangladesh, like some women in the West, have come to realize that they too understand the message of Jesus and feel compelled to share it through preaching?

The last two definitions of "full participation" addressed the roles of deaconess and priesthood. The notion of women performing either of these ministries was so new that less than half responded. Many did not understand the concept of deaconess. Almost two-thirds of the small minority answering did not feel that equal opportunity to be a deaconess should be included in the definition. Twenty-eight percent felt that equal access to priesthood for women is integral to the meaning of "full participation." Of these, significantly more were Tribal and single women. Perhaps, given the church's law on priestly celibacy, only single women feel that priesthood can be an option for them. Sisters might also be expected to support priesthood for women, but to the contrary, only a small minority do. This attitude could be a result of the training they received from the congregations which formed their spirituality, most of which are European in origin and maintain a traditional understanding of the church, the priesthood and religious life (see Appendix C).

Three additional questions related to ordination for women shed further light on how Bangladeshi Catholic women feel about this controversial topic. Even though less than a third see priesthood as essential to full participation, 41% said they would like to see women ordained as priests. When asked if they themselves would like to be trained for ordination, 25%, the majority of whom were single women and women under 40 years of age, indicated they would. Fifty-seven percent would not seek ordination for themselves and 18% expressed indifference. About two-thirds of the total surveyed said they would be willing to support other women desiring ordination.

The various responses regarding ordination reflect some inconsistencies, but it should be remembered that before this survey the concept of women's ordination was unknown to many of these women, particularly those in the villages. When the questionnaire was distributed among the Tribal women, they indicated that the idea of ordination for women had never entered their heads. However, they are talking about it now!

How do Bangladeshi women feel about the issue of their equality both in society and in the church? Ninety-eight percent of those answering believe that Jesus Christ wants men and women to be treated equally. It is important to note that almost all of these Catholic women attended "mission schools" administered and staffed by sisters, both foreign and Bangladeshi. These are women whose role is to proclaim the church's mission. Perhaps the ears of the Bangladeshi girls were opened by these women, to hear the "Good News" of Jesus' message of equality. Given the culture of the country, one can't help but wonder what the percentage would be if this question had been asked of Bangladeshi men.

The central issue is not whether women are aware of their "non-personhood" in the church and in society, or even if they want to be ordained to the priesthood, but whether the Catholic Church is fulfilling the mission of Jesus in regard to women.

> The mission of Jesus is summarized succinctly in the Gospel of John. "I have come that you may have life and have it to the full." Jesus meant fullness of life for all, not just for half of the human race.[10]

The answers to the questions relating to the mission of Jesus, and how women in Bangladesh perceive that mission and their role in it, revealed a depth of understanding and a yearning for justice on the part of many. There were some women, however, whose limited level of awareness precluded their ability to envision any role beyond that traditionally allowed them by the church.

The responses were evenly divided on the question "Do you believe that the message of Jesus regarding the equality of women is being lived in the Catholic Church today?" Those who believed that it was cited the same few examples repeatedly:

> Our church cares for the poor and destitute.
> The church shows love and pity toward women.
> It gives us spiritual help and advice.

These responses illustrate the limited level of expectation these women have regarding their equality in the church (see Appendix C).

Those who felt the message of Jesus was not being lived indicated numerous ways in which women are not treated as equals:

The church says we are equal but does not show it in practice.

Our church is like a pyramid, I'm at the bottom and I don't receive any equality.

We read about respect for women in the Bible, but I don't experience it.

The church does not walk side by side with its women.

More highly educated women, sisters and women living in cities readily expressed their awareness of the failure of the church to fulfill the mission of Jesus in regard to women today.

The observations made by these Bangladeshi women are reinforced by Malladi Subbamma when she says:

All religions have opposed either directly or indirectly the concept of equality between the sexes in the domestic sphere as well as in the sector of morality. In one breath, the religious pronouncements run thus: "All men and women are equal before God." Do we come across any woman officiating either as a priest or a person leading the prayers, whether it be in the temple, mosque, church or synagogue? No, she is not fit for the job. She is there to serve only. That is why she is debarred from playing a significant role in places of worship.[11]

In spite of their experiences, over 96% of the women indicated they believe Jesus Christ wants his church to treat women as equals with men. Eighty-five percent feel that they deserve to be treated as an equal by their priests. For women to feel they deserve equal treatment and to experience it are two different things. The highly educated women were significantly more aware of their unequal treatment. There is a correlation between the heightened level of awareness that results from education and the understanding of what it means to be treated as an equal in the church.

It is encouraging to note that 83% of those who responded in Bangladesh indicated that they identify with other women of the world who struggle for equality within their church, and almost 95% identify with other women who struggle in society. In addition, 94% said that they would like to learn more about women who are struggling with them. Some of the things they felt they have in common with women in other countries are:

We are all deprived of opportunities and the freedom to think and act in the church.

We are all willing to fight for our rights.

We have a desire to improve the church and our mental health.

We are all independent, progressive, free-minded, and have a sense of justice and want leadership.

Two women of neighboring India, describing the structure of their church and their disillusionment with it, support the feelings of the Bangladeshi women previously quoted.

Benedicta Ageira says:

Presently the structure of the church has not only deprived women from equal participation by giving them inferior positions but also a small group of clergy has accepted the bondage of being superior to a large group of people who form the body of Christ. As long as this situation persists there can never be communion in practice in the church, for there cannot be communion between unequals.[12]

and Flavia D'Souza states:

I wish the women in the Catholic Church would form a union and stage a walk-out.... I am tired of a worship that fails to recognize my existence. . . . To be a woman in the church means to be invisible. . . . We have no say in the formulation of canon law . . . our spirituality does not shape doctrine. And theology based on our God-experience is dismissed as "feminist nonsense."[13]

As of now, no Bangladeshi woman has articulated the status of Catholic women in the church so graphically. However, it is obvious from the data that these women share a great commonality with oppressed women in the church around the world. They are voicing their hopes for the future—hopes that are joined to those of Catholic women everywhere.

Will those hopes be fulfilled? Will the church treat women as Jesus did and give them, not crumbs from the table, but the very Bread of Life?

> Only to the extent that the church at-large—men as well as women—continues to commit itself to the struggle for full human rights—and for the full equality of men and women in the church and society alike—can we conclude that there is any substance to this hope.[14]

Meanwhile, the song of the Bangladeshi women, *"Shoono! shoono! shoono!—*Listen! listen! listen!" continues to call us, women and men of the church everywhere, to hear what they are saying about their dissatisfaction with their status in the church, and their desire for more active participation. Will the church, hierarchy, clergy, men and women as well, hear their call?

The women of Bangladesh who are awakening to their oppression pray with Rabindranath Tagore, the Bengali poet, who assures his people that their struggle for freedom will come to fruition:

> [We] are destined to bear this burning flame
> [in the burnt-offering fire].
> O my mind, bear this burning pain
> but harken to the call to unity;
> Fight on and win out
> no matter what the shame, the dread;
> Pay no heed
> to dishonor and affronts.
> This intolerable pain
> will come to an end one day
> and a vast new life will be born. . . .[15]

4

RISE UP WOMEN!

Brazilian women emerge

Where shall we find a liberated woman?
In the public square,
in the corridors of power,
in the pulpits,
and in our midst.
She dares to stand up for freedom,
not only for her gender,
but for all who are oppressed.[1]

In 1990, Catholic women's groups in Brazil proposed that the motto for the annual Lenten campaign be: "Rise Up Women: Your Liberation Is at Hand." However, the motto chosen by the bishops "Woman and Man: Image of God" moved the focus of the campaign away from women's oppression. The response of women theologians and pastoral agents was immediate.

"In itself, the choice speaks loudly of the fear of openly dealing with a crucial issue," says Eunice Buoro, who works with women in the Archdiocese of Goiania. Catholic theologian Ivone Gebara observes, "The churches are afraid of bodies, principally women's bodies. They are afraid to open up spaces because this will demand a new organization of 'sacred' space and power." Rosa Adela Osorio, a member of a theological reflection group in Sao Paulo, challenges, "The church should be the first to accept full participation of women if it truly believes in the example of Jesus. Unfortunately, instead of being a prophetic voice in relation to women, the church is way behind."[2]

Women theologians and scripture scholars all over the world are pointing to the example of the way Jesus treated women in his day and are asking, "Why doesn't the church follow the example of Jesus?" In Luke 13:10-17, the story is told about Jesus curing the woman who had been bent over double for eighteen years. She immediately stood up straight and glorified God. And that, says Maria de Groot, can only happen after you are raised up. "You can participate in the community where only men have leadership and can speak, but you do it as someone who is bent over and distorted. Only if you are lifted up by the power of Jesus does your own song awaken."[3]

A parallel can be drawn to the Brazilian women of today who, like other women of the world, have been bound not for eighteen years but for over eighteen hundred years by the power of patriarchy. They are beginning to realize that Jesus freed them from that evil long ago, but church leaders have prevented them from rising to their full height. Nevertheless, women have begun to sing their own song and participate in their own salvation as they lead 80% of the basic Christian communities. This is what liberation theology is about! What tremendous work is being done by these formerly bent over but now straightened women. Yet this structure does not leave them room even to begin to stretch to their full height. Is the institutional church so fearful, does it have so little confidence in the power of Christ that it doesn't want all God's people to stretch to their full height?

In a recent interview, a Fairleigh Dickinson professor of the sociology of religion asked, "If God loves women as much as men, why does the church reserve its ministries and higher responsibilities to men?" A Brazilian theologian observed:

A woman can conceive a priest, physically and spiritually: her motherly example can one day result in her child's becoming a bishop. But she herself can never be a priest or a bishop. What good will it do to have a theological theory of women's liberation (Gal 3:28) if oppressive practices persist in the church?[4]

Brazil, the country

In order to begin to comprehend the situation of Brazilian women in the church and society, it is important to have some understanding of this vast and complex country. Brazil is comparable in size to the continental United States, with a population of approximately 155 million, 89% of whom call themselves Catholic. The majority of the people, 75%, live in cities, while the remaining 25% live in the rural countryside or in the *favelas* on the periphery of the cities.

This survey of over four hundred Catholic women encompassed the urban and rural areas of the south, east and northeastern regions of the country, where dramatic differences are evident. The people in the southern region, most of whom are descendants of European immigrants, are generally more affluent and better educated, while those in the northeastern states, the descendants of African slaves, are less literate and among the poorest.

The national life expectancy for both men and women is sixty-four years and is affected by education and wealth. It varies from fifty-five years in the northeast to sixty-nine in the south. Sixty-eight percent of the people nationwide, 45% in the northeast and 88% in the south, are literate. However, many of those classified as literate can only write their name.

A high percentage of Brazilian people are of mixed race, i.e., Indian, African and Caucasian. Black African slaves were at one time the majority. The distribution of ethnic groups at present is approximately 54.8% White, 5.9% Black, 38.5% Brown and 0.6% Yellow.

In the words of one Brazilian priest, "Brazil is a rich country of poor people." Nearly half the population, over sixty million, live in extreme poverty. Ten percent of the people own 80% of the land, while forty million are migrant, looking for jobs. The richest 1% receive as much income as the poorest 50%. The minimum salary is less than $50 a month and 40% earn even less. However, 50% of the people are under fourteen years of age. These children are the country's greatest potential and greatest challenge.[5] A large percentage of children are precariously holding on to life in the midst of poverty and drugs. Of one hundred students who enter first grade, only twelve will finish secondary school and only six will enter the university. According to recent statistics, black children born on the east side of the city of Sao Paulo are more likely to die in a shooting than enter the university.[6]

Women's reality in Brazil is one of oppression on almost every level of family, society and church. Brazilian society is characterized by "*machismo*," a Hispanic form of male dominance and aggressive behavior. Men are free, willful and powerful, while women are subject to limitations of all kinds, ranging from male control over their private lives to their restricted position in society.[7] Women are invariably considered in relationship to the home. Even though they are present and fulfill important roles in the home and society, they are invisible because their presence does not count.

Women are often seen as non-persons in society, oppressed by a father, then abused by a husband and finally deserted by a son. In reality they become daughters without fathers, wives without husbands and mothers without sons. Without a relationship to one of these male figures, they are "no one."

In her book, *Against Machismo*, Elsa Tamez interviews fifteen male Latin American liberation theologians (six of whom are Brazilian). She asks them all the same question, "Is the oppression of women real?" Her premise is:

> If Latin American men do not recognize the reality of women's oppression, if they do not admit that they are promoters or accomplices of the ideology of machismo that permeates our culture, if they do not realize how great the riches that are lost to society due to the marginalization of women, if they do not move from theoretical conviction to liberating practice, if they do not join in solidarity with women in their struggle, the path of the feminist movement in Latin America will be longer, the progress slower and often more bitter, with more frustrations than joys.[8]

Nearly all theologians interviewed made reference to the fact that reality in all its dimensions is affected by the oppression of women.

Pablo Richard indicated that the ordination of women would be a signal that the transition from a Christendom model to a church of the poor is being accelerated.

> Christendom is a macho structure. . . . In the church of the poor the structure is not one of power but is rather

communitarian. Women have been able to participate in the church of the poor, and at the same time women's participation has led us to discover a new model of church. . . . Women's participation in the church is extremely important if we are to move from Christendom to a model of the church of the poor.[9]

As women's awareness of themselves as persons of value increases they begin to stand on their own feet to break the patterns of macho tyranny in their home life.

I was born a woman and have to look at myself differently and not say, "I'm only a woman."

To free ourselves from *machismo* women have to be aware, to be conscious we are equal and fight for it.

You have to be assertive even in the way you walk.

Today, because of the severe economic conditions, Brazilian women must work outside the home if they want their families to survive. In the religious arena, many of these women also serve the larger community as animators and leaders of base communities. Women are also bringing this new awareness to the church which has reinforced the system of *machismo* by teaching women to be submissive. The faith of these women is telling them that God does not will that they suffer at the hands of men.

The Brazilian church

A background narrative of Brazil is incomplete without a description of the Catholic Church and its people. Even though almost 90% of the population claim to be Catholic, many feel that all the churches are the same and participate in Catholic as well as spiritist, pentecostal, evangelical and African-based religions depending on convenience and what feeds their souls. There continues to be an extreme shortage of priests to minister to these millions. Official statistics indicate 1.8 priests for every 10,000 people, and the ratio is dwindling.[10] Unfortunately some of the hierarchy and priests, particularly the Brazilians, are aligned with the rich land owners. They oppress the poor and are against the rich land owners. They oppress the poor and are against the base community movement because it enables the poor to stand up for their rights against their oppressors.

> The emergence of the basic church communities in Brazil began with a community evangelization movement in Barra do Pirai [in the Rio de Janeiro district] and the efforts of lay catechists there. . . . In 1956 Dom Agnelo Rossi initiated an evangelization movement, using lay catechists, for regions of Brazil not being reached by pastors. . . . The basic communities mean building a living church rather than multiplying material structures.[11]

During the 1960s, the basic Christian communities began to expand in the rural areas and poor neighborhoods on the fringes of the cities of Brazil where people rarely were visited by a priest. Parishes in these areas may average 150,000 people served by one or two priests. Because of the shortage of priests, Catholic sisters, drawn to the needs of the poor, became pastoral agents and animators of these communities. The communities are just what the name suggests, a gathering of people (predominantly women) in neighborhoods often in a hall built by the cooperative efforts of the members. The communities are not actively connected to the parish though they are technically a part of it even though some resist parish limits. The people in the communities tend to view the institutional church as the dispenser of the sacraments, i.e., baptism, marriage, and the sacrament of the sick. The sacrament of reconciliation does not play an important role in their lives. They are more attuned to the social doctrine of the church than to its moral directives, which they rarely hear. One priest remarked, "We can't get around to teach them all anyway, so we let them act according to their consciences. Ignorance is bliss!"

"What do the people in the base communities seek?" According to Jose Comblin, "They seek charity; that is, they want to rediscover what is most central to Christianity and to put the church back into the life that is lived daily again."[12] Perhaps that is why women feel so comfortable participating in these communities in leadership positions. They have found a space to put justice and charity into practice and be recognized and treated as equals in their church community.

Catholic theologians speak of the obvious marginalization of women in the church. Boff considers it "a historical sin." All of them acknowledge the exclusive control of men in administration and governance with no theological or biblical justification. Nonetheless, *all of them* happily mention the central role of women in the CEBs [basic Christian communities]. Because of its communitarian structure this new model of the Latin American church allows for a significant participation of women, which is not to be found in the official institutional model.[13]

It is evident, especially to the inquiring visitor to Latin America and to Brazil in particular, that a new model of church is being born of the people. Women are finding a place in that church where they are coming into their own and are making portentous contributions. As their participation increases, the anti-feminist stance of the institutional church is becoming less and less credible. In fact, there is no justifiable reason for excluding women from full participation in the ministry of the church today. Maria Clara Bingemer gives support to this with examples from the early church:

> The historical Jesus initiated an itinerant charismatic movement where men and women worked together as partners. . . . In addition to preaching about the kingdom, Jesus' movement was characterized by joy, a lack of prejudice (all kinds of sinners and marginalized people were welcome at meals and celebrations) and its disregard for many of the societal taboos of the time. . . . The idea that women are part of the kingdom and that they are called by Jesus, not only as contributors but as active participants as well as privileged beneficiaries of his miracles, is found in all four gospels.[14]

Women in the base communities are clearly active participants and they are looking forward to the time when they will be the privileged beneficiaries of true equality in their church.

The majority, 70.3%, of the base communities are in rural areas and in poor neighborhoods on the outskirts of the cities.[15] Because people in the cities, except on the periphery, find places

73

outside the church to fulfill their social needs, they do not ordinarily belong to a small community, but attend the parish church in the traditional manner. Many women indicated to me they just stop going to church when they do not find the nourishment they seek or when the priest is perceived as seeking power over them. Others, put off by the challenge of socially conscious priests to change their lives, go to the evangelical or pentecostal churches where the services are more emotional and provide them with a warmer and safer sense of community. The bishops of Brazil are aware of and concerned about the lack of participation by urban Catholics. The bishops realize they have not yet reached them or responded to the needs of urban Catholics in the way the base communities have responded to the needs of the poor. However, in 1991 under the leadership of Cardinal Evaristo Arns, a great effort was begun to establish base communities in the cities also.

Brazilian women's view of the church

The term "practicing Catholic" has a variety of meanings for Brazilian women. For those in the base communities, the institutional church only touches their lives when the priest comes around every month or fortnight to preside at the liturgy. The remainder of the time the community is the church! Some attend the meetings and prayers of the community, but do not receive the sacraments. Others, particularly the men, consider baptism the one and only requirement for being a Catholic and do not participate in any formal way. The greater majority do not consider attendance at weekly Mass with a priest an essential part of being a Catholic. Most likely this is due to the fact that Mass has never been available to them on a regular basis, so when it is available few men attend.

Participation as eucharistic ministers and lectors in their weekly "culto" (para-liturgical service), or in the case of urban women, at the liturgy, received a favorable response. Seventy-four percent said they would like to be lectors, many of these added the qualification, "If I could read!" Over 36% of those responding were illiterate. In their eagerness to take part in the survey they brought their literate daughters to read the questions and write the answers for them. Almost 57% indicated a desire to be eucharistic ministers. For some the question was not only whether they wanted to be a minister, but also whether the members of the base community chose them to be one! Eucharistic ministers are elected by the members of the community. Others felt they were not worthy to perform this ministry.

Eighty-one percent indicated that their hopes for the inclusion of women in the Sunday *culto* or Mass are fulfilled. The reasons given were: "In my community, women can take part if they choose. There are more women readers and eucharistic ministers than men. Our liturgy team has a majority of women, and women direct the Sunday service in the absence of the priest." Since the majority of those answering (over 58%) are members of base communities where women are the organizers, leaders and main participants, these were expected responses. Others remarked that they have the opportunity to participate and, "If they don't, it is their own fault!"

The reasons given by the 19% who did not feel included in their Sunday liturgy ran thus:

Women are included only because men don't want to assume subservient roles.

The homilies only express the men's point of view.

Women's participation is very limited.

Women are only included in "theory," not in real life.

Only sisters value women not priests or other men.

Others do not attend church at all and did not answer this question.

The response to the question, "Do you believe that Jesus wants men and women to be treated as equals in society?" resulted in an overwhelming yes from 98% of the respondents. Their reasons were powerful in their simplicity:

We are all children of God and therefore, all equal!

We believe that we are equal to men and that Jesus wants us to be, because the sisters taught us that we are. We didn't know it before!

Other questions relating to equality revealed the feelings and perceptions of these women living in a macho society. Eighty-three percent feel that they are in fact equal to a man, while only 29% say that men treat them as equals. When asked if they wanted to be treated as equal to men, over 92% indicated that they would. Thus, 63% of the women desirous of equal treatment are not receiving it. Women in one of the *favelas* commented:

> Neither our husbands nor our children treat us equally. We have value only in the kitchen or in bed.

> Why do women have to be quiet when men speak? If we are human beings, why the difference? We should be treated with respect because of the qualities we have.

> Women have an obligation to put an end to what the men do to them, otherwise, they will continue to do it without end!

Unfortunately, most women are not putting an end to what men do, but are in many cases, reinforcing their macho treatment. This is illustrated by Goldsmit and Sweeney in their account of Latin American women's struggle for equality and justice:

> Paradoxically, women themselves are an obstacle in the path of change because of the religious and social conditioning that makes them accept as their moral obligation the defense of the established order, whether political, religious or social. In defending the status quo, they transmit to the next generation a tradition that allows only a limited and defined role for women in society, a role that demands submission and passivity.[16]

Some of these poor women in the *favela* have discovered that, through trust in one another and faith in their God, they will find a new way. When women come together to share their pain and their joy, they feel valued. They are slowly beginning to realize that in their culture, it is women who give value to women, and together they have strength. One woman expressed it with conviction when she said, "With faith in Jesus, we will win and change our situation!"

Among the obstacles women feel they meet in their efforts to achieve equality in Brazilian society, *machismo* was mentioned most frequently. Nearly 68% of those answering put it at the top of their list. Other obstacles indicated were social customs, family tradition, lack of equal education and economic necessity. The women were eager to talk about them:

> Only when you have some money, can you talk back to your husband on an equal footing.

> When women start making money, husbands often taunt them with trying to *be someone!*

> Fathers feel that girls should not be educated because they will only write notes to their boyfriends.

> My husband won't allow me to go anywhere that requires staying overnight, even to a church-sponsored conference. He doesn't trust me.

This last comment is very characteristic of Brazilian men regarding their wives and daughters.

How do these women who are so oppressed in their society feel about their situation in the church? Their response to whether they think Jesus wants women to be treated equal to men in the church was a strong 98% yes. A little over 61% think that Jesus' message regarding women is being lived in the church today, while over 38% feel it is not (see Appendix C).

The majority of these women are members of a base community where men do not actively participate. They have a greater sense of equality and participation than women in the traditional parish.

> The church encourages us and allows us to participate in all the activities of the base communities.

> I participate with men in decisions, have freedom to give my opinion and am usually heard.

> I am respected for my work and as a catechist.

In traditional parishes, rich women often contribute to the domination of poor women. An example of this would be when poor women are invited to "participate" in church festivities. Their participation consists of cooking for the celebration so that the rich can enjoy themselves. Class snobbery is very obvious in parishes. The poor are looked down upon by the upper classes when they go to the parish church, while they are accepted as equals in their own base communities.

Those who do not see the church living the message of Jesus responded:

No, the church does not treat women as Jesus would because it only considers women for those jobs or services that priests or men don't want to do!

No, Jesus treated everybody as equal, but the church does not.

We don't have the same rights as men in the church, we don't have decision-making power or full participation.

It's only out of stubbornness and determination that women have any say in the church.

The bishops and priests only let us do the leftovers!

One woman summarized it well when she said, "Women are being valued today in the Catholic Church for no other reason than their work. In general, men don't frequent religious functions nor do they accept serving as catechists."

To demonstrate how the Brazilian church devalues them, the women described the church's widespread practice of baptizing girl babies with the name "Maria de Jesus" and omitting the record of a family name. Girls are not considered significant enough to record their surnames. The baptismal registers in parishes have literally hundreds of "Maria de Jesus" listed!

The institutional church and the Vatican are far from the everyday lives of the rural Catholics who find God in their community. The community supports them, helps them fight for justice, sustains them in prayer and is the place where God is present among them. Most of these base communities are animated by sisters who personify the church for them. One woman expressed it well. "I wish I could deal with the priest like I do with sister, we can sit down and talk together like equals."

Women have not yet come to the point of speaking up to the priest or the bishop because of many years of conditioning that "Father is always right." Or, because the bishop has that title, he deserves submission regardless of who he is or what he does. One Brazilian sister told me that she has come to the conclusion that she must treat the institutional church like every other bureaucratic institution, with its laws and structures. "The real church," she said, "is the church of the people!" Sonia Alvarez speaks to these two concepts of church:

> The Brazilian People's Church has empowered women as citizens, encouraging their participation in community, yet . . . the church's inability to cope with women's empowerment as women, the inevitable by-product of such participation, severely circumscribes the future direction of women's participation in the church and community life.[17]

Does this description of church depict the same church Jesus founded? The church, in all its members—bishops, priests and laity—is called like Jesus to perform deeds and acts of liberation which are signs and proof of the presence of God's justice and mercy in this world. Where are the signs and the proof of the presence of God's justice in the institutional church's treatment of Brazilian women?

The fact is that a strong wind, a new Pentecost, is blowing through the women of Latin America in the base communities. They are speaking in new tongues, seeing with new eyes, hearing with new ears and taking new steps. They are raising their voices in hope that their song and lamentations might be heard.

The institutional church has seemingly turned a deaf ear to the plea of women for liberation, acceptance as equals with men, and improvement of their human condition. . . . Those women who actively seek justice and liberation in Latin America often encounter a church that largely ignores their problems; it does not adequately understand or accept their anguish or their struggle.[18]

The institutional church, personified in the bishops of Brazil, made a preferential option for the poor at Medellin in 1968 and again in 1979 at Puebla. This church has yet to prove that this option specifically includes women, since women are the poorest of the poor! Until it does, women are neither free nor equal. These daughters of Abraham and Sarah, unable to stretch to their full height, will continue to suffer from their infirmity. If the church is sincere, and honestly wants to implement its option, the bishops will hear the lamentations of the women and put their words into action. To fail to do this is to betray the mission of Jesus.

How do Brazilian women define "full participation" in the church for them? Fifty-eight percent of the women speaking about this topic are members of base communities in which "full participation," except for the roles of deaconess and priest, is part of their life experience. That is, leadership and decision-making positions are open to them. They can be lectors, homilists and eucharistic ministers. On the other hand, 42% of the women belong to traditional parishes in which these roles are considerably limited for them. Approximately 65% of those answering feel that to participate fully, women must have equal decision-making power with men as well as equal opportunity to be eucharistic ministers and lectors. In regard to equal leadership positions 53% indicated this was included in their definition. Forty-five percent saw equal opportunity to preach the homily as part of their understanding of full participation. About 39% perceived the role of deacon important to the definition, and nearly 46% felt that priesthood for women is essential to the meaning of "full participation" (see Appendix C).

Other questions relative to priesthood for women, which was a new concept for most, drew the following comments:

The sisters do all that the padres do, so why shouldn't women be priests?

It would be better for us women!

No, because women don't keep confidences.

We have a woman mayor so why not?

People have it in their heads that men are priests and women are servants.

Some women felt that ordination would be too much responsibility at this time. Others laughed because they were

80

either married with children or were old, a presumption that celibacy and youth, not maleness, are requisites for priesthood.

In response to the question, "Would you like to see women ordained as priests someday?" 69% said they would, 10% would not and 21% were indifferent. Given the opportunity for ordination, 28% said they would like to be trained, and over 94% indicated that they would support other women who want to be trained (see Appendix C).

To what sort of priesthood would these women be ordained? Leonardo Boff strongly emphasizes the fact that, "Women neither can nor should simply replace male priests. They should articulate their priesthood in their own way."[19] Elizabeth Gossman reiterates:

> Let us be quite clear that a woman is simply not suited to ecclesiastical office as we know it today. Only when it has been transformed from within, and reconstituted in relation to the community as a whole, might it become something transferable to women.[20]

Brazilian theologian Frei Betto contends that "in the base communities, where we see a new church arising from the people, women play the same roles as men."[21] Obviously, women have already begun that transformation and reconstitution of the priesthood and are preparing for that transfer!

Women comprise over 80% of the membership of the base communities. It is a church of women! They prefer the small communities to the institutional church because in the base communities there is more unity and opportunity to participate. If these opportunities existed within the parish church, women would feel welcomed and valued as they do in their communities.

The concern in rural areas is that so many Brazilian priests are overextended and do not know how or do not care to be one with the people. They go to the communities once or twice a year to offer Mass and administer the sacraments, and have to leave without establishing any relationship with the people. Consequently, many communities prefer not to have the priest come! The danger is that Brazil will soon become a priestless people, a people who perceive they worship better without a priest who neither relates to them nor values their participation. According to Boff:

> The ministerial priesthood is not a power to consecrate; it is the power officially to represent the one, eternal priesthood of Jesus Christ. . . . The priesthood of Christ does not posit its specificity in the power to consecrate, but in being the principle of unity in the community. A woman can exercise this *diakonia* as well as a man.[22]

It is evident that they are doing so already. It would seem that Brazilian women in the base communities have achieved a fuller participation in their church than have other women in Brazil and the rest of the Catholic world. Since very few men participate, women are in fact "the church." When asked if they identify with other women who struggle for equality in their church, over 72% said yes.

In a society where *machismo* dominates women's whole lives, their struggle for equality is even more apparent. Men are clearly present and have power and control over women. Eighty-two percent of the respondents indicated that they identify with other women who struggle as they do, and over 95% indicated that they would like to learn more about these women. On the positive side, some of the values and sentiments they feel they have in common with women who have taken on this battle for equality in other countries are: "We are all fighting for justice, respect, freedom, greater participation, a better world, a recognition of our gifts, intelligence and free will." On the other hand: "We are fighting against discrimination, oppression, disrespect, injustices, inequality and the power that men have over us." It is evident that these women desire more rights and privileges in their society, and 87% indicated they do.

Similarly, 77% said they would like to have more participation in their church. This high percentage indicates that neither women in the base communities nor women in the parishes are satisfied with the limited amount of participation presently afforded them in their church. They refer to quality rather than quantity, because the majority stated they would not have time to participate more even if they had the opportunity! Most women work outside the home and, on the whole, their husbands find it beneath them to share in the household tasks, thus women have very little free time even to go to church.

As was mentioned earlier, Jesus' attitude toward women was one of reverence for their dignity and equality, but along with Leonardo Boff we question:

> Will the church be able to live up to the stature of its divine founder and receive from him the critical yardstick for its own understanding of woman?

> In a world where woman is discovering her identity, can the church be a factor for liberation?[23]

The answers to these questions are yet to be proclaimed. In the meantime, sisters and other lay women continue to walk hand in hand toward that vision of church that embraces all of humanity as Jesus intended. Through the mutuality of their pain and oppression, and the realization of the strength and power they have when they support each other, women are rising up in spite of the institutional church's refusal at this time to follow the example of Jesus in their regard.

Who is the strength of a liberated woman?
Her God, her family, her friends,
for she grows by their affirmation, and succeeds
through support and a helping hand,
all the days of her life. Amen.
Yes, let us say: Amen![24]

*"The church tells us men and women are equal,
but if women cannot raise their arms
to consecrate bread and wine,
we are not equal!"*

—a Ugandan woman

Part 2

WOMEN CHALLENGING THE CHURCH TO LIVE THE MISSION OF JESUS

5

HOW LONG MUST WE WAIT?

U.S. women question

How long, O God, must we wait
before our faith comes to fruition?
How long must hope keep vigil
at the doorposts of despair?
How long must those passed over
pass the time in expectation?[1]

Catholic women in the United States are tired of waiting. Two thousand years is a long time to anticipate the fulfillment of the church's baptismal promise that, ". . . there is not male and female; for you are all one in Christ Jesus" (Gal 3:28). Many women in today's church echo the words of Barbel von Wartenberg-Potter.

What should women say about two thousand years of men's sermons other than: "We cannot go on like this. Your exclusiveness, your sermons, your way of being church, does not mean anything to us women anymore; it certainly does not mean enough." Women still do not have the power to mark the examination papers of the men's church and write "failed" across them. But unfortunately, as so often, people vote with their feet. Many, far too many, are leaving to go into no-body's land, the land of the goddess, because it is better than the desert where they are hungry and thirsty.[2]

Women are angry and hurt when they witness the institutional church's acts of oppression, its injustices, its lack of inclusive liturgy and its outright discrimination. One woman spoke of the hypocrisy practiced in her suburban Maryland parish when the local bishop came to offer Mass. "We ordinarily have altar girls as well as boys, both women and men lectors and eucharistic ministers," she said, "but not when the bishop comes. God forbid that he would think that a woman would dare to tread upon the carpet of the altar!"

A Filipina-American woman spoke of the rejection she suffered from her parish priest. She and her husband had attended all of the classes required in preparation for the diaconate. At the end of the course her husband was ordained and a celebration dinner was given, but she was not invited. The priest said to her "Jack is invited because he is an ordained deacon, but you are not." Her angry reply was, "I'd rather not be a priest if you are an example of what priesthood means."

The church cooperates in maintaining the values in society which militate against women. At its deepest levels the institutional church does not accept women as full-fledged human beings. A former parish minister observed, "We're either pedestalized or we're put in the gutter." She then went on to speak of her experience of working with priests in a parish:

> They didn't know what to make of me, but they didn't want to get too close. A woman is always a great temptress to them. I was either a saint or a sinner. I wasn't a person they could act naturally with, who could be morally responsible for myself and others.

Such experiences raise a question regarding the kind of training priests receive in the seminary. Shielded from women as they are, some lack the interpersonal skills required to relate to women in the ordinary ministerial or social situations they encounter in a parish setting. Seminary faculties comprised only of men contribute to such paranoid behavior. A highly educated, well qualified woman theologian who applied for a teaching position in a seminary was told that she would never be hired simply because she was a woman.

Middle-age and older women in America who have volunteered their time and expended their energy for the church in myriads of supportive ways, hoping for more opportunities, are now tired of waiting. "I don't do parish work anymore," one woman remarked. "If I support a dysfunctional system it will continue to be dysfunctional, so I won't do it anymore." Another told how she left her parish because she couldn't become what she felt God was calling her to be in that environment. "I stopped going to church for the first time in my life," she said. Then a friend invited her to join a small community of twenty families who meet in a public school building, select their own celebrants and include women in their liturgical celebrations. "The bishop knows we exist. He doesn't like it, but there isn't much he can do about it."

Another woman spoke about her eighteen-year-old daughter's attitude toward the institutional church.

> She is ice cold toward the church. She knows I participate in a community outside the diocese. She has no interest in the sacrament of confirmation. "Why?" she asks. "I'm not going to be an adult in the church no matter what ceremony I go through!" I can't find it within myself to tell her otherwise.

A mother of five girls described her dilemma in trying to respond to her fourteen-year-old daughter who wanted to know where her place is in the church.

> My daughter asks why she can't be an altar server, why she can't serve in the church. What do I tell her? How do women tell their daughters, in this "age of women" that there is no place for them in the church? How do they tell them that Catholic woman are expected to sit in the pews and keep quiet because if they try to stand tall and participate, they will only hit their heads on the hierarchical stained-glass ceiling?

A woman who struggled with her own daughter's questions had this to say:

> It's almost ludicrous that young girls cannot even carry a cross or wash a priest's hands as an altar server, yet women can distribute the eucharist. There are dioceses where this can be done. If you don't make a fuss, they look the other way.

Women in a midwestern parish did make a fuss! All of the religious education teachers went to their pastor and offered him a choice, altar girls or their resignations. They had altar girls the next Sunday.

Two women, one a sister, spoke of how they had felt called to priesthood from the time they were ten years old.

> I never thought that by the time I was twenty-five or thirty that I wouldn't have the opportunity to answer that call. I find it so incomprehensible at times, that it can't be. I have to tell myself all the time, this is the way it is, it can't be! I want to invite people into my pain.

> I am forty-five years old and I too felt that call when I was ten years old, but I didn't say it because I thought everyone would laugh. I was told that little girls don't become priests, they become sisters.

The sister then went on to express the pain she had been living with for thirty-five years. "I say to God, why did you call me to this ministry in a church that won't let me in and won't even acknowledge the legitimacy of my call? To deny this call is like telling me I don't have brown eyes."

In a similar vein, what do you tell a seven-year-old who wrote the following to her parish priest?

Dear father
Sulena I wish I
was a boy so
I could be a
alter boy
and help you
ordapriest
just like you
I can't wait
until I make
my firstcommu
nion. I will be
7 prettysoon
my Bithday is on
April 24
Love
Lauren

90

The desire for equal participation in the church often begins with the age of reason and continues as a little girl grows in awareness into womanhood. However, the church's arguments for excluding females who feel called to participate are far from justifiable. Marcello Azevedo, S.J., poses the question:

How can we explain the fact that the church has not carried into practice the formidable liberating message of the gospel: that all human beings, as children of God, share in the same dignity and enjoy the same rights?

The church that led its children to accept martyrdom as a witness to their faith was not capable of applying the gospel that abolished all discrimination based on sex to its own structures as well as those of civil society upon which it exercised decisive influence.[3]

Other scholars contend that once it was clear to the early church leaders that Jesus' second coming was not imminent, they felt free to return to their patriarchal treatment of women which continues even until today.

"What the Catholic Church needs," says Richard McBrien, theology professor at the University of Notre Dame, "are progressive groups that push the fast forward button on the ecclesiastical VCR." Some women's groups are doing just that and want to offset other groups who McBrien describes as being "stuck on the rewind mode of that same VCR, trying to return to pre-Vatican II days."[4]

The challenge of inclusive ministry

Women's groups today are calling the church to conscience, to live what it says, to practice what it preaches about justice, about equality, about the sins of sexism, discrimination, division and exploitation. Perhaps, as one woman noted, "Women are not screaming loud enough. We've been trained since infancy to keep quiet. It's important that we stop being intimidated by the clergy." Another put forth her plan of action.

I don't back away from any opportunity in the church. Women have to be ready when openings come. We need to volunteer for everything, whether to give a homily or lead a discussion. We can't wait for our children to do this. The church moves slowly. We can't wait another twenty years.

A businesswoman from Gary, Indiana moved to a very practical level when she said, "Maybe we're going to get around Rome with the money issue. It's the only thing that talks." Many women all over the country spoke to the fact that they no longer contribute to a church that gives lip service to its message of the equality of men and women, equality of person, and equality of rights. The question they pose is a valid one, "Why is it that the right for women to answer God's call to full ministry is not included in the church's definition of equal rights?" American women control significant amounts of money and are beginning to see how it can be used to further their cause for equality in the church.

Another area where women feel they can no longer wait is in regard to liturgies that fail to nourish them. An artist in Virginia who said she hadn't heard a good homily in twenty years was challenged not to remain passive by a woman who offered an alternative from her own experience.

> I'm not sure we have a right to continue to go along with services that fail to nourish us. I think we do have a choice. We have to search and find what nourishes our faith life. We can't operate as people unless our spiritual side is nourished. I'm going to stay in the church only as long as I can find a community and a liturgy that is nourishing for me.

To see more and more people denied participation in the sacramental ministry of the church not only saddens women, it angers them. As Michael Crosby, O.F.M., so aptly put it, "The preservation of the male, celibate, clerically controlled model of church, the maintenance of patriarchal clericalism in Catholicism, has supplanted the message and mission of Jesus Christ."[5] Women certainly deserve more. Yet they are reduced like the Canaanite woman to pestering the church:

. . . pestering for the sake of their daughters and for themselves. The church has a choice now, as Jesus did then, between dismissing such women as pests or listening to the nagging questions raised by women and hearing them as an invitation to respond to its own vocation more fully.[6]

Jesus did not dismiss the Canaanite woman; he ultimately gave her what she asked. It is true that he did not give in easily or without argument. Her begging and pleading raised his awareness to the fact that his mission was not just to the tribes of Israel, but to the whole world. This poor pagan woman, by her faith, her logic and her perseverance, was able to help Jesus see his mission in a broader and more inclusive sense. American women in our time have that same faith, logic and perseverance. Will the church hear them and respond with a fuller vision of Jesus' mission today?

Bishops in the United States have been listening to what may seem to them to be the nagging voices of women. Some few, like Jesus, have heard this cry for justice and full participation in the church for women and their daughters. Others, through suspicion, contempt, fear or weariness, dismiss these women as pests hoping they will go away and stop bothering the hierarchy.

But the questions won't go away even if the women are ignored because they are basic to the mission of Jesus. Are the Pope and bishops more sure of what Jesus' mission is than even Jesus was? Why is the hierarchy so afraid to listen, to open their minds to the possibility that perhaps they do not possess all of the truth?

Jesus listened, argued and came to understand the wisdom of the Canaanite woman's argument. He was not tied to his own opinion. He was courageous enough to go against the traditional and sacred Jewish understanding that the Messiah was sent only to the "Chosen People." Jesus' action poses an even more important question for us today. Can the preservation of a male priesthood possibly be more traditional, more sacred to the hierarchy's understanding of the mission of Jesus than justice and equality for women as full participants in that mission?

Jesus related to women as persons with worth and dignity. In this story as elsewhere, Jesus is seen as capable of a critical stance toward a women and respectful of her self-affirmation as she boldly counters his own remarks.[7]

Sister Teresa Kane, S.M., hoped for the same critical stance and respect from John Paul II in Washington, DC, in 1979. In recalling the Pope's own concern for human dignity, she asked him to provide the possibility of women as persons being included in all ministries of our church.[8] Unfortunately, she too was dismissed and humiliated as a pest.

Women who struggle for equality in the church do so because they believe Jesus envisioned the church as a seamless garment without patches. They believe that it is only when men and women together provide the warp and woof for weaving that garment that Jesus will recognize it as truly his own. Until that happens, there will be loose threads and large holes which will continue to prevent the church from bringing that vision to fulfillment.

Women who are crying out for justice and equality may seem to the hierarchy to be as pesky as the Canaanite woman. Nevertheless, for women the issue is not a question of eating the crumbs that fall from the clerical table but rather, of breaking the Bread of Life, a ministry to which both women and men are called. How long must they wait to hear the hierarchy say, "You are women of great faith! What you want will be done for you" (Mt 15:28, *Today's English Version*).

> It's an irony, isn't it, that the only people we know who actually handled the earthly body of Jesus were women. They were at his birth and his death, at his cradle and his tomb. And yet the only people not now allowed to consecrate the sacred elements of Christ's body and blood are, again, women. And behind the prohibition lies deeply hidden the fear that somehow the female brings defilement into the holy place.[9]

Women have had two thousand years of indoctrination in the Catholic Church. They have made a great investment yet get the least return. Women have no voice in decisions or policy making, no opportunity to share in ordained ministries, yet they are expected to obey all the laws of the church made by men.

Women's greatest sin in the church may well have been humility and submissiveness. But today women in greater and greater numbers are stepping out of the mold they have been cast in and are calling others to do the same. They are tired of waiting but, remarkable as it seems, many still live in hope.

> There are women who believe that the prophetic Spirit of the Bible has not ceased to be at work—after all, it was poured out on sons and daughters (Acts 2:17-18)—but that it will free the church from her patriarchal inflexibility through the unpredictable way in which it will blow, whether softly or with consuming fire.[10]

A sister whose ministry is the training of men for the diaconate had this to say "I keep pushing the boundaries. Let's go for it, let's try it rather than being pushed by them." In her ministry she seeks to empower laywomen. "Once they get the language and the vocabulary the church will never be the same!"

Women not involved in ministry and who are content to remain in the pews, think they are treated as equals in the church. They do not seek anything and so they are not even aware of the obstacles they would encounter if they did. "I don't know how you can miss the oppression," said one woman who seeks total involvement in church ministry. "It is everywhere at every level."

A young black single mother in Los Angeles voiced her observations strongly. "If we sit and sit, nothing will happen. Every parish should organize and the women should make their voices known. Then some changes will come about."

A Hispanic woman pointed out that women need to be invited. "If we want to make a change in the church we have to ask more women to participate. Women bring kindness, caring, peace and gentleness, and maybe even more understanding."

"I think women in the parishes need to come forward more," said a middle-class professional woman. "In my parish the councils are all male. Women need to put themselves forward for these positions because no one is going to ask them."

What have the efforts of women over the past thirty years accomplished for them in the church? They have moved from full-time in the pews and part-time in the sacristy to full-time in the pews and, with a few exceptions, part-time in minor ministries in some parishes. What gives them hope? Why do they remain in a church that continues to exclude them? What makes them think they will ever be welcomed as equal ministers and full participants in the church?

Tenacity for hope

Some who are truly at the doorposts of despair take strength and inspiration from the story of Jesus casting out the evil spirit from a man. The man was convulsed and then sat peacefully. These women work with great energy toward casting out the evil spirit of patriarchy from the church. They realize that many will be convulsed, their whole being will be torn apart, but the end result will be peace and true communion for men and women alike in the church.

Women who have experienced pain and humiliation from local clergy and hierarchy, who cannot endure the injustice and hypocrisy any longer, are losing hope. Some are finding consolation in participating in services conducted by women in other Christian denominations.

If the spirit of ecumenism that began in Vatican II teaches us anything, it is that we can learn from people of other faiths, that we Catholics do not necessarily have the whole truth of what Jesus taught. A Catholic woman in Pittsburgh whose parents were Episcopal and Presbyterian expressed her amazement at the loyalty she finds among other Catholic women in the face of such oppression and shared her experience:

> Somehow the shortcomings I perceive in the Catholic Church I find fulfilled in other denominations. When I go to these other services I find these women being treated wonderfully by Episcopalian women priests. I am amazed that more Catholic women don't find themselves taking a look elsewhere in other churches.

A woman in Los Angeles who is also an Episcopalian shared her feelings of inclusion when she experienced a woman presiding at her service.

> Some years ago I was in a church where there was a woman minister. It wasn't that different from a man

minister except I felt more included. I felt she was my own. Then I became an acolyte. I felt so included. If women could participate more, they could change the church.

A Lutheran woman who was working with sisters for the first time indicated how surprised and impressed she was to find so many powerful women, administrators, professors, doctors, etc. She questioned "Where are they? Why aren't they prominent in church ministry?" She was deeply impressed by their knowledge and opinions and observed with a certain pathos:

I'm feeling that the Catholic Church in some way is throwing their female energies away because there are all these women with strength, but they don't have the space to work, to express themselves and show what they can do. I think it's a little bit sad.

The women quoted have experienced in their respective churches an openness toward the fulfillment of their baptismal promises. They do not have to wait any longer! When their churches say to them, "There is not male and female; for you are all one in Christ Jesus" (Gal 3:28), they make an effort to bring these words to life. Hearing their stories, it is not hard to understand why some Catholic women are weary of waiting for the same fulfillment.

Women of faith find hope in the communities where they minister and in the inner conviction of God's call. One woman liturgist from Ohio described how she depends on the affirmation of the community she serves, "I don't think that the gifts that flow out of me would be the gifts they are, if I was not called."

If you have the inner call, part of the test of the call is the affirmation of the community. This is where the power of the Spirit is, as well as the hope. That's what keeps me going, the affirmation of the community. At this point I function as best I can, hoping that the young women coming behind me will reap the benefits.

Women all over the country spoke about their inner strength and the growing numbers of women responding to God's call today.

My oppression is that I feel I cannot follow my call to ordination. Women who are called are women of great integrity, theologically prepared, faithful, gifted and who love the church. We want our call to be discerned and there is no vehicle for this to happen. This is an injustice to the church, the women and to the people they would serve. Even as this oppression continues and escalates from Rome, the heartening thing about it is that more women are studying and responding to their call as best they can.

It is extremely difficult for these women to keep faith and continue to have hope. What does spur them on are the results of the recent Gallup Poll indicating that growing numbers of Catholics, 67%, support the ordination of women to the priesthood and 80% favor women as deacons. These women believe that the "*sensus fidelium*," the faith of the People of God, will prevail so they continue to hope. Whenever we hope in other people we strengthen them and make their burden lighter. When women sense that other women and men as well share their hope, they will feel buoyed up and will have courage to continue in their struggle of challenging the church.

They that hope in the LORD will renew their strength,
they will soar as with eagles' wings;
They will run and not grow weary,
walk and not grow faint (Is 40:31).

6

BREAKING THE SILENCE

Bangladeshi women speak out

How can [we] keep faith
when deliverance has been so long
in coming?
How can [we] keep confidence
when there is no sign
that You are near?[1]

Characteristic of many Catholic women of Bangladesh is their unspoken anguish about their role in the church. It is a suffering that very often is not clearly identified, even among themselves, until put to the question. Then very slowly the veil is parted and the silence is broken! Their voices are still a whisper in comparison to their Catholic counterparts in neighboring India, but loud enough to be heard by those who will listen. However, it would be extremely difficult today for Bangladeshi women to challenge their bishops as did lay theologian Astrid Lobo Gajiwala when she spoke to 120 Catholic bishops of India in January, 1992. Gajiwala openly warned the bishops that women are losing patience with the official church and its apathy toward their problems. "As a prophetic church, we are called to lead the way in the struggle for gender justice. If the church machinery cannot work with us," she warned, "we will reappropriate the church and work for change ourselves."[2]

We might well ask why it is that Catholic women of India are apparently stronger, more outspoken and more actively working for equality in the church than women in Bangladesh. The

99

most obvious reasons include: a freer Hindu cultural background, greater educational opportunities, and the numerical strength of Indian Catholic women. Catholics in India are 2% of the population (approximately seventeen million people) and the women have strong ecumenical ties with other Christian feminists.

Catholics in Bangladesh are small in number (180,000) and the women live under the strong, oppressive cultural influence of Islam where women have been veiled, secluded and silenced for centuries. The ecumenical feminist movement is just coming to birth. Many Catholic women are still strongly influenced by the Bengali proverb: A woman's heaven is under the foot of her husband. Submission is considered the cardinal virtue and as a result, women are beaten, tortured and even murdered by their husbands with impunity.

Unlike Indian Catholic women, it is only during the past twenty-five to thirty years that Catholic women in Bangladesh have been encouraged or permitted to attend college in any numbers. In 1967, the topic for debate between students from a men's college and a newly founded women's college illustrates the prevailing mindset: "Higher Education for Women Does More Harm than Good." This attitude toward women's education increases the burden on women who struggle for educational opportunities even to this day. Comprising such a tiny minority in a totally male milieu, women lack a much needed support system that would enable them to speak out publicly on behalf of women's rights in the church. Because they do not have that support, many women are afraid to say how they really feel.

A prime example of such fear is a college educated, happily married village woman, who lived for a year in the United States and had been exposed to feminist views of the church. When asked to discuss women's oppression in society and the church she prefaced every response with the words, "In general, we are speaking in general." She was unable to say "I think," or "this is my situation." Since everyone is known in the village, the fear of something she said getting back to her husband or to the parish priest, prevented her and others in the group from freely expressing themselves.

That same fear is expressed in the women's attitude of "peace at any price" in the home. "Women must have patience and not disagree with their husbands," is the message communicated in various ways. The same holds true in their parish. In one parish when women had begun distributing communion objections arose among some of the parishioners. The women themselves settled the dispute by withdrawing and agreeing that only sisters and brothers would assist the priest. When necessary others would help, but not out of a sense of a call to ministry. Peace was established in the parish, but at what price? Lack of strong leadership and fear of confrontation caused the women to give up a ministry they had every right to perform.

Many of these same women said they feel equal to men in their church participation because they are free to go to church and pray with their husbands (even though they sit on opposite sides), while Muslim and Hindu women are not. Their understanding of equality is derived from measuring their rights and privileges against the predominant Muslim mores and is therefore extremely limited.

For the most part, Tribal women feel satisfied with their participation in the church. As relatively new Christians, with little experience in the institutional church, they are still exploring the riches of the message of Jesus as they come together to pray each week. However, they are learning what it means to be a woman in the church in their infrequent encounters with clerical oppression and domination. Similar to women in the basic Christian communities in Brazil, Tribal women are leaders in their matriarchal society as well as in their church.

Voices of sorrow, frustration and anger

Women in villages and cities throughout Bangladesh describe their feelings of hurt, rejection, humiliation and anger as they speak about the minimal role allotted to them by their church. They realize their oppression does not come from foreigners as much as from their own Bangladeshi priests and bishops. "These are young men who have come from our own villages and families. If they are extraordinary, how come we are not? We received baptism and the Spirit as well, shouldn't we have equal opportunities?" A sister described how she had worked ten years in a certain parish and a new young priest was appointed pastor. She knew the people, the customs and practices of the parish. "He came in just like a king, acted as if he knew it all and didn't consult me on anything. In our culture" she said, "we show respect to our elders. Somehow, this training is lost in the seminary."

Many women spoke to the fact that only a few laywomen have been given "permission" to be lectors and eucharistic ministers and for the most part, only sisters have been called to these roles. "Sisters are not more holy than we are" said one village woman. "A sister is a person, we wives and mothers are persons too. We can do what sisters are doing." Many Bangladeshi sisters who take on this preferential role may not be aware that their behavior is creating yet another division in the church and it is the other laywomen who are challenging them.

A city woman spoke of her feeling that Protestant women are far ahead of Catholic women because they can move forward in their churches in ways not yet open to Catholic women. Protestant churches are already discussing the issue of women's ordination at the parish level. An Anglican woman commented, "We are trying to shake the very root of the church's structure, and are coming into collision with people who do not want to give up their power and prestige."

Several sisters and other laywomen shared their experiences of both priests' and bishops' treatment of women in the church. A sister, who has worked for twenty years with women, related a painful experience. She had asked the bishop if he were aware that almost 90% of the Catholic women in his diocese are beaten by their husbands. His reply was, "I'm sure that for the most part they deserve it!" Nowhere in the Bible do we find Jesus speaking about women with such contempt. Yet priests who treat women like servants or children, or at best second class citizens, often cite biblical reasons for their actions.

In a workshop for married couples conducted by the same sister, a man who had been married for twelve years revealed that his marriage had been "hell." "Until now" he said, "I didn't realize that I was the cause of it!" As a result of the workshop he promised to change his attitude toward his wife. The sister related that her efforts on behalf of women were bearing fruit in these workshops, but so far she had not been able to reach the priests.

Sisters are among the best theologically educated women in Bangladesh, yet feel unappreciated and dominated by the clergy. They gave examples of their sorrow and frustration.

In the church, the sisters are respected only for their work. As long as you work without questioning you are fine and good, but if you want to give your opinion, it is never accepted. Sometimes they take your idea and fulfill it as their own, never giving you credit for it.

Sisters are not allowed to take classes in the seminary so the priests often humiliate us in a parish setting by saying, "You don't know. I studied this in the major seminary and am more knowledgeable."

Both sisters and other laywomen became very animated when they talked about their hopes for women in the church. A thirty-two-year-old Bengali sister, who ministered among the people in the hill tracts of the north, shared her reflections.

Before, I was not for women priests. I didn't think women should be priests. But now, with my living experience my idea is changing and I say yes. Women would be good priests and homilists. Women have a natural gift to give homilies. For the last two years we have had no good homilies at all.

At the other end of life's continuum the same desires were expressed by a seventy-four-year-old woman who has ceased attending Mass. She didn't have to think a minute before reeling off a litany of what she would like to do as a woman in the church. "I'd like to light the candles, read the gospel, give the homily, distribute communion and I'd even divorce my husband, if need be, to be ordained!"

Other women spoke of wanting to bring communion to the sick, serving at the altar, baptizing, anointing the sick and burying the dead. There is a diversity of opinion on whether women would make good confessors. Some agree that women can't hear confessions because the men will say, "Women can't keep secrets," or "If the women hear confessions they'll tell everything." Others strongly asserted their belief that "Women can hear confessions! Men will talk, but let them talk, they won't bother us!"

"I'd like to be a bishop" said a former sister who is presently active in addressing justice issues in the country. "Bishops often don't do what they say. They speak about injustice but there are many injustices in their own lives. If I were a bishop," she continued, "I would try to live what I preach."

Others spoke of the need for both laymen and women as well as sisters to give homilies because "the priest doesn't speak to the reality of the people. We get bored hearing from the same priest day after day. If the father or mother of a family could speak from his or her experience, the homily would have more meaning." Another observed that "the gospel is not alive in the church, because the priests don't prepare their homilies."

Women who wanted more spiritual nourishment from other women spoke to their realization that even if women could give homilies today, the men wouldn't pay any attention to what they said. They also observed that "if a few women would begin by just giving a five minute homily, it would be good and the men would slowly begin to listen."

Expressions of women's gifts

A woman from a small village in the south of the country told how she came to realize that she was capable of ministering in the church equally with the priests and sisters. She related how one of the sisters had shown her a book of ritual for funerals, marriages, baptisms, etc., and explained how to use it in case the need should ever arise. Much later when the priests and sisters were all away at a meeting in a distant city, a man in the parish died and there was no one to bury him. She remembered the book, went to the convent, got it, prayed over the body at the grave, sprinkled it with holy water and buried the body. When the priest returned, he blessed the grave. What impressed her was that she, not a man, had been chosen for this important responsibility.

In a parish where the pastor and the sisters work together to involve the people, a basic Christian community was started in each of the four villages comprising the parish. After some time the parish council made the decision to change the community structure to neighborhood blocks. Each block has seven husband

and wife teams in charge of training the children for receiving each of the sacraments. The parish priest and the sister are very active in training both men and women well for their catechetical responsibilities. The women are very pleased with their new role and they credit one of the sisters in the parish for bringing them to an awareness of their gifts and value as women. "If sister hadn't come," said the leader of the group, "we would not be in this position, we would still be in the dark!" At the same time they feel frustrated because they want to do more. The leader of the group identified the prime reason for their frustration, "Because we don't have a shortage of priests in Bangladesh," she observed, "we can't even do what women in other countries are able to do." These women have yet to realize that opportunities for them to minister should not depend on the number of available clergy but rather on their God-given gifts.

Vocations to the priesthood and religious life are flourishing in Bangladesh. The six dioceses have more than enough priests and sisters to meet the needs of the small Catholic population of 180,000. Added to the fact that the church has not yet felt the need of additional lay ministers, men or women, is the pervasive Islamic cultural oppression of women. Therefore, Catholic women in Bangladesh are struggling for the opportunity to minister in the same ways that many other women in other countries already take for granted.

A group of sisters in a parish were sharing some of women's concerns with their parish team, particularly the fact that many of them said they would feel more comfortable confessing to a woman. The men showed great surprise at this information. When asked how they, the men, would feel confessing to a woman, the light of understanding dawned in their eyes. For the first time, they had a glimmer of the pain women experience in the patriarchal church. In a country where women find it humiliating to go to a male doctor to heal their bodies, they are forced into the same humiliation by the church in order to heal their souls.

"The heart of the gospel is at stake as long as the church remains male-dominated and lopsided," was the observation of an Anglican woman whose own church is addressing this issue. It is true that not many Roman Catholics in Bangladesh are discussing the issue of women's equality openly, but some women are. "If women can do everything from riding a cycle to being prime minister, why can't we have the opportunity of being a priest?" asked a woman from the hill tribes.

Bangladeshi women also see advantages for women to become priests.

Women priests would free us as women to tell our sins and share our life.

It is very difficult for a woman to confess to young priests.

Sisters can easily relate to the people. People feel free to talk to them, they accept them. Sisters have a thirst for the word of God and the eucharist but cannot quench it. Priesthood would do that for them.

They also spoke of the problem of young priests hearing the confessions of young girls, and indicated that scandal and misunderstanding frequently come from this. Others articulated their need for a more pastoral approach by the priests.

If there were women priests, I would go quickly to one and talk over my problems.

The priests today never have time to get to know us, they come, offer Mass, and go. Women priests would take more time with us.

Women are good thinkers, very creative. Women priests would be very meaningful in the lives of the people.

Still others spoke of the trouble that would arise if women were ordained and of the time it would take for the majority to accept women in that role in Bangladesh society. However, they also indicated that in places where people are more educated, women priests would be accepted much more quickly. One woman felt that priesthood for women is a long way off because women are still struggling for small rights in the church and, more importantly, priests won't approve of women. Another asked a most provocative question, "What does the church have to fear from a handful of women moved by the Spirit to follow a call?" Indeed, the church does have a lot to fear, not from women but from its own blindness says Chitra Fernando.

A church which refuses terms of complete equality to half of the human race should not be surprised to find that it has become increasingly irrelevant in the world of today.[3]

Many of women's attitudes regarding their role in the church are a reflection of how they see themselves in their society. Almost all Bangladeshi Catholic women consider themselves far better off than Muslim or Hindu women. This blinds many women to the reality of their oppressed situation. Others realizing their helplessness, because of lack of education, financial dependence or concern for their children resort to the "peace at any price" tactic. They submit to the humiliation of being a servant to their husband's every whim.

Because Bangladesh is a "dry" country, the Christians resort to making homebrewed beer, wine and whiskey. Drinking is often a big problem with men. Wives are not only subject to beatings from their drunken husbands but are also expected to work hard to either brew the liquor or provide money for their drink. This sometimes means resorting to prostitution which the husband accepts without question as long as it is for his benefit. Many women believe it is their responsibility to be patient and accept whatever the men do, hoping that as a result, they will be treated equally!

Obstacles to change

It is obvious that most Bangladeshi women are not initiators of change, primarily because of their culture. However, when an idea is presented to them, they don't ignore it. They may hunger for more than crumbs, but often the bread has to be set before them before they realize the depth of their hunger.

Women with some education spoke strongly to the need for both husband and wife to be educated. "Otherwise, men will always think they are superior and will never accept us." They also acknowledged that earning money gave them a voice in the family affairs. Financial independence along with a sense of their own worth are the greatest aids to equality.

Unfortunately, some women prove to be stumbling blocks to others. Because they themselves were mistreated by their mothers-in-law when they were young, many older women in turn put obstacles in the way of their daughters-in-law when they want to go on for education, or to attend awareness workshops. Having waited so long to be "on top" the mother-in-law becomes the oppressor in order to enjoy her power.

The same is too often true in the church. When a sister spoke of her frustration of being on the parish council and not supported by the other woman on it, she was told that it was because of jealousy. "We do not like other women getting ahead," said a leader of the group. "There is such a lack of unity among women. If we could unite we could do so much more toward getting equal rights." She then went on to explain another reason why women are not united. "In the church there is no large organization for women. There are a lot of small clubs and committees that are good, but keep us divided." "The priest won't allow us to do anything for women," chimed in another active woman. "He gives all kinds of excuses temporizing until the moment passes."

A highly educated woman, who travels extensively to other countries of the world, spoke about the effects of her own Bengali culture on women:

> We as women are not respected. The culture degrades women and keeps us second class. I am a woman and the universe is my country, but when I return to Bangladesh, I feel suppressed as a human being.

She went on to give an example of the cultural restriction in her country against women traveling alone.

> After coming home from a trip abroad, I visited my mother in the village. She insisted that someone accompany me to church, a short walk through the village. Since no adult was available, she sent a small child with me. I was angry and had to ask myself, who is protecting whom?

The matriarchal Tribal women in Bangladesh expressed their feelings of oppression in different yet sometimes similar ways. Tribal women inherit land, are often more educated, more ambitious and more apt to take leadership than men. However, this does not automatically make them equal to their husbands, nor are they considered the head of the family. The man does, in fact, rule his home and the woman asks his permission to leave it as Bengali women do.

In recent years, Bengali people have moved into Tribal areas, taken over their lands and asserted themselves as the predominant culture. As a result, more Tribal boys, seeing the advantages of the patriarchal system for them, are becoming educated. The men are beginning to revolt against the matriarchal system which gives inheritance rights to women. Some are choosing to marry Bengali girls who come from patriarchal homes and tend to be much more submissive than Tribal women.

Outside the home, however, Tribal women have been the leaders in the church as well as in society. Since Tribals compose the majority of Catholics in Bangladesh, there is hope that these women will instill courage in other women to speak the unspoken, to challenge the unchallenged and to change the unchanged in the hierarchical and patriarchal systems that continue to silence them.

A sign of hope for many is the belief statement and efforts of an ecumenical group of women in Dhaka, the capital of Bangladesh.

> We believe that the fate of the oppressed has to change if the human race wants to survive on this globe. We are convinced that this survival does depend on the breaking down of all barriers between men and women, rich and poor, people of different races and cultures. With this vision we look at the Bible, at the gospels, and see that this is what Jesus was about on this earth.[4]

This group's method of theological reflection is helping to build awareness among Christian women from different denominations. The ecumenical center provides a stimulus for workshops and study courses on the Bible and theology for women. It offers counseling services on home and family relationships to help women learn to be more assertive about themselves and better prepared to challenge the injustices perpetrated against them in family, church and society. The courage of these Christian women, who represent only .1% of the population, indicates the depth of their faith.

Catholic women in Bangladesh who hunger for more from their church, can be likened to the sower in the gospel who went out to sow the seed. Surely some will fall by the wayside and be trampled on by men. Some will fall on rocky ground where there are few who will support and nourish it. Some will fall among thorns of antagonism and fear. But some will also fall on good ground. The seeds that have been sown are small, but these women are hopeful. They are venturing into the work of moving the mountains of oppression and prejudice against women in the church. They believe in the words of Jesus, "If you have faith the size of a mustard seed, you will say to this mountain, 'Move from here to there,' and it will move" (Mt 17:20). Imagine what these women will be able to do with the support of women around the world as that mustard seed sprouts and grows into a mighty tree.

There is a great deal of hope and anxiety for the future in the hearts of Bangladeshi women. These feelings are fittingly expressed by Rabindranath Tagore in his prayer for freedom.

> Where the mind is without fear and the head is held high;
> Where knowledge is free;
> Where the world has not been broken up into fragments
>   by narrow domestic walls;
> Where words come out from the depths of truth;
> Where tireless striving stretches its arms toward perfection;
> Where the clear stream of reason has not lost its way
>   into the dreary desert sand of dead habit;
> Where the mind is led forward by thee
>   into ever-widening thought and action
> Into that heaven of freedom, my [God], let [our women]
>   awake.[5]

7

OUT OF THE KITCHEN

Ugandan women come forth

Be confident, you who are tentative.
Her Spirit-Force is with you.
Throw off the inner and outer ways
of submission and subservience.
Look up and look life straight in the eye
and do not cringe before it.
Take charge of who and what you are
and what you intend to be.[1]

Everywhere in Uganda, in towns, villages, cities and universities among the poor as well as the not so poor, women are proclaiming the same message. "Our president has called us out of the kitchen and given us freedom!" The women are excited, energized and enthused about this new opportunity to take charge of their lives. They are rising to the challenge! For the first time in their memory there is support from legitimate authority to cast off the heavy shackles of their cultural heritage—the chains that bind women exclusively to the kitchen, to child care and to the garden.

However, things are not totally idyllic and opinions vary regarding what that freedom really means. As previously mentioned, the government now invites women to run for public office. Women can even rise to the post of chairperson of the various councils. As one woman sagely pointed out, "Yes, it is correct. We are free and people can vote for us, but the men *will not* vote for us!" Another added, "Most women are fearful to stand for office; they are far less educated than the men, and they don't feel qualified." The more educated see it as a beginning, but admit there is precious little one woman can do on a council when she is so outnumbered. "A woman, no matter the position she holds in the community (or in government) still remains a woman, meaning she is a second-class human being."[2]

When asked how their husbands feel about women becoming involved in politics, responses were both positive and negative. Some men still do not want their wives outside the home. Husbands are suspicious of their wives' intentions and think they might go and roam about neglecting their work at home. Others indicated that cooperation does exist between some husbands and wives who arrive at an understanding that allows the women to "leave the kitchen." Still others spoke of the husbands who beat their wives if they leave home without their permission. Many of the women interviewed, who clearly see their chance to "leave the kitchen" as a sign of women's freedom, still accept wife-beating as their due. Perhaps the opportunity to move outside the home will give them a greater sense of their own dignity as women along with the insight and awareness needed to withstand such abuse.

Most of the women interviewed felt assured that their president is recognizing their worth and is calling them to stand on their own feet. However, many men are fearful of losing power and control over their wives. One of the ways some women are coping is the age-old game of subterfuge. One older woman said, "We have to get our husband's permission subtly. We have to let them think they rule us, that they are superior and are head of the house. Once we get involved, the men will understand." Because of poverty and ignorance, freedom to act without fear of reprisal is still a long way off for some women of Uganda.

How many women worldwide deceive and debase themselves and the men in their lives with this type of behavior? Feeding the men's ego so that they will "allow" women to do something they have every right to do serves only to intensify the power men have over women. This happens repeatedly in every society and is exacerbated in the Catholic Church.

The present government has been in existence in Uganda only since 1986 and the constitution providing for women's participation in politics is very new. Therefore, it is only recently that women have been appointed as ministers and elected to other positions of power. They were previously denied such opportunities to use their talents. "In the future, you will see that Uganda will have a president who is a woman," foretold one enthusiastic respondent from the rural area. Another from the north emphasized this prediction, "Now, when we have opportunities to use our gifts, our country will be better for it." A young nurse summarized the feelings of most women interviewed by saying, "We have not yet achieved equal rights, but we want to be equal." Although 70% of the women questioned indicated they wanted to be treated as equals to men, only 5%, the smallest percentage in the four countries surveyed, said they felt they were treated equally. This indicates that Ugandan women's awareness far exceeds their experience.

The initiative taken by the government on behalf of women's political rights is helping women see that all cultural norms are not necessarily for their benefit. In discussing why they as women do not feel equal to men in their society, women referred to some practices still present in the villages, but for the most part not evidenced among educated urban women. One such custom is that of girls and women kneeling before a man when they speak to him, especially a parent, an employer or a person of rank. This obviously puts the woman in a submissive and subservient position and conveys a strong message to the man, "Here I am, do anything you want with me!" Because of strong cultural support and their lack of education, women subject themselves to this type of humiliation over and over again.

Women were also divided over the question of freedom of speech in their society. Some felt there was great improvement for them, that women are now free to express their ideas in gatherings when men are present. Others pointed out that though this might be true in the town, the majority of village women do not feel they can speak openly at all. Women cannot give their own views when a man is talking, they are expected to sit and listen. It is only the educated women who have the right to speak. One woman noted that her mother would not even sit at the table with a man in the village let alone speak with him. Village women stand in the doorway and listen, remaining on the periphery while men speak. A married village woman cannot even eat with her husband, she only cooks his meal and serves him. He may, if he feels generous, give her a few pieces of meat from his plate. In addition, as part of the culture, some of the more nourishing foods and delicacies such as chicken, eggs and grasshoppers are reserved for men.

Many of these customs stem from the fact that a woman is indeed the property of her husband. He literally buys her from her father at the time of their wedding. The bride price is negotiated between the men; women have to accept whatever is arranged. In addition to selling his daughter, the father often uses the dowry money for the education of his sons. The bride becomes the property of her husband and if there is trouble in the marriage, cannot go back to her parents because she has been bought! A childless woman whose husband divorced her after thirty years, was taken to court so he could demand the return of his bride price. Her parents, having eaten the goat which had been the bride price, were already dead. The woman had nothing, neither children nor home, but was called by the court to pay!

A Ugandan woman has no parental or property rights. Her husband owns everything, even the children are his exclusively. If a woman works outside the home, she must hand her salary over to her husband, and when he dies, she is left with nothing.

One Ugandan sister explained the growth in her own awareness and that of many women who were educated by western missionaries. "Our culture is responsible, girls are brought up different from boys. We were taught to believe that women are lower than men. Our education has helped us understand we are not lower and we are changing our attitudes."

Others spoke of the responsibility of the educated women to raise the awareness of the village women to their oppression. "We need to tackle the issues of domination and submission that are embedded in our social, political and economic institutions," remarked another woman, "not in a conflictual way but to promote women's status." This awareness of educated women of their responsibility toward one another, provides the wedge that will widen the crack the government has made in their cultural mores for more and more women to step through to freedom. Ugandan women are imparting a strong message to women in other countries, "In unity there is strength to liberate women from unjust oppression."

The government of President Museveni has proclaimed loudly its intent to improve the condition of women, even to the extent of going against the culture. Some women described his effort thus far as "calling them out of the kitchen and giving them their freedom." Others viewed his attempt as a beginning on the long road to freedom.

The patriarchal wall

What has the church proclaimed to women? Do women not deserve the same commitment from a church that preaches the mission of Jesus? When will the church, in the person of the bishops, call women out of the pews to the sanctuary? It is very discouraging to note that instead of a liberating message the church continues to hold women captive and regards them as second class. Until now, the church has been unwilling to act counterculturally in its fulfillment of the mission of Jesus. We look in vain for the cracks in the patriarchal wall because women are eagerly waiting to step through them to equality. Ugandan women do not hear the hierarchy calling them out of the pews to full participation in the ministerial role of the church. Unfortunately the voice of the church on behalf of women's equality remains inaudible.

The same Ugandan women who were so enthusiastic about their government's call and support, spoke sadly and dispiritedly about their church. They referred to the fact that, on the whole, women are given menial jobs such as cleaning the church and cooking for functions. The only areas in which women are allowed to be leaders are in their own groups and committees or in the choir. Men lead everywhere else and make the decisions as well. The example was given of women participating in the parish council with men. "When we come to the meeting, the men have already met and decided things ahead of time. We really have no voice." Like their counterparts in Bangladesh, Brazil and the United States, Ugandan women encounter the same patriarchal oppression in their endeavors to minister in the church. "At present men see themselves as leaders of everything. They don't give women chances and privileges." One woman gave an example, "When a person is dead, a woman is not even allowed to lead the burial rites."

Some few women, most of whom are sisters, have been allowed to be trained as catechists. One young woman explained, "They are doing wonderful work and the people love them, but the rest of us are not given the chance." Another woman noted that she sees a distinct division between what men and women are allowed to do in the church. "We have no altar girls and laywomen cannot distribute communion or give a homily, even though many could do these ministries better than men." Two sisters from different communities articulated their pain in being excluded from church ministry:

> In the church there is no equality. Women can't do anything, can't give homilies, and have no responsibility to be ministers. Only men can do things. I'd like to feel I'm part of it!

> When I am given more opportunities to participate as a woman, I will realize that I also belong to the church and the church wants me to serve! Since we are all equal in God's eyes we hope for much more.

Women's feelings and awareness are epitomized in the statement from the Association of the Religious of Uganda relative to the upcoming African Synod:

> As an association of women, gathered to make a statement and offer our contribution to the African Synod, and aware of our responsibility for the proclamation of the gospel, we are aware that what we submit will be almost exclusively interpreted and dealt with by men. We therefore feel the need to state that: The oppression of women in practically every aspect of life—social, cultural, political, economical and even ecclesial—is a reality. To neglect to deal with these issues or to diminish the importance of these questions would be a further grave injustice to women of Africa. We have noted the almost complete silence on this subject in the *Lineamenta*.[3]

From the pews to the sanctuary

When these same women were asked what they would like to do in the church that they are currently prevented from doing, their whole attitude changed. They became animated and excited at the prospect of doing more meaningful ministry. Their entire focus was not on what ministry would do for them but, rather, on what they could do for the people and how they could help spread the Good News. "We have to differentiate between equal opportunity and equality," observed one young woman. "We can't be equal physically to men but we can have equal opportunity."

One young sister related her unusual experience of ministry to prison women. She had accompanied a priest to the prison where he offered Mass for the women prisoners and she had been asked to give the homily. The women told her afterward how pleased they were to have another woman speak to them at this time in their lives. Unfortunately, most priests do not invite women to respond to such an obvious need as these women prisoners. The desire for women to minister to women as homilists and confessors was expressed repeatedly by Ugandan women.

Another described the effect that three young women trained in the new school for evangelization, had on an old man in her village. "I've never understood my faith like this before," he said. "These young women have made me hear the word of God!" Then he asked the question, "Are they any different from a priest? They too are preaching the word of God." The woman telling the story then added wistfully, "It's too late for me to become a priest, but not for my daughter!"

Many others spoke to the need and desire of women for theological training and preparation for sacramental ministry. "There are so many people in the villages who die without the sacraments because there are no priests. We could respond to their needs!" Some talked about the paucity of spiritual food they receive in the homilies they hear in the church. "I would like to preach. Maybe because I am a teacher, what I say would be more convincing." They observed that if both men and women were allowed to preach, there would be better homilies.

Women talked about the serious problems of teenage pregnancies as well as the threat and reality of AIDS. "The priest cannot stand in their shoes as we women can. We could certainly minister to them more empathetically."

An even greater concern for those interviewed was the fact that women are barred from teaching in the seminaries. They feel that women's presence would help the seminarians learn how to interact and relate to women so that when they work in parishes their behavior would not become a scandal to the people. Evidence of the truth of their concern was given by a group of sisters who chose to move away from their parish church. The pastor was taking money from the people for both drink and women, clearly not imaging Christ for them. These sisters chose to have a communion service each morning in their own chapel rather than participate in the daily eucharist in the parish.

Women of all ages and social strata spoke about the advantages of having the opportunity to become priests. Their reasons were simple and compelling:

Women comprise the great majority of church-goers.

There are not enough male priests to minister to the needs of the people.

With the ordination of women, more people would be served.

Women are devoted and faithful; they are not afraid of work.

I think it would be good if those who are committed are ordained. Our sister-church is doing it!

Another woman added, "The Protestants are better than us, they can be 'reverends.' For us, we can be missionary leaders or sisters—only that!"

As R. Modupe Owanikin says:

The priestly vocation is usually the result of God's call. . . . The importance of the call is that it is God who takes the initiative of choosing persons for the priesthood; the initiative is not dependent on human discretion. . . . For men to exclude women who believe they are called by God to the priestly ministry would amount to limiting God and replacing God's will with human will and prejudices with all their errors and inconsistencies. On this basis, the ordination of women to the priesthood should be taken for granted.[4]

The women continued to speak about the injustices women suffer in a male dominated church. "The church tells us men and women are equal, but if women cannot raise their arms to consecrate the bread and wine, they are not equal!" Women are gifted, but their gifts are exploited or buried. Sisters who devote their whole lives to the church are denied the opportunity to be sacramental ministers. One young woman reminded the others of the beginnings of Christianity when women like Lydia had house churches, "Maybe women could do that again," she said.

Susan Muto expresses the conviction of these women and all women of faith:

> Women who believe do not need proof. We know that Jesus Christ has confirmed the dignity of our personhood and called us to the fullness of discipleship. It remains a scandal to many that even now we are not afforded the rights and respect men in the church and society take for granted.[5]

The fact that Ugandan women expressed many reasons why they could or should be ordained does not indicate they were unaware of some of the problems that would result from such a departure from tradition in their church. The women acknowledged that the greatest hurdle would be men's resistance to women priests. They also spoke about the need to raise the awareness of all people to the injustices of clerical domination and to the ministerial gifts women are eagerly waiting to share. They were clearly aware of the conflicts that ordained women in Protestant churches are experiencing as they struggle to respond to the spiritual needs of their people. In spite of and in addition to all of this, they could say with confidence, "It will come! Change always has opposition, but this can be overcome."

So these faith-filled Ugandan women wait to be called from the pews to the sanctuary. Even the least educated are aware that the government is doing more for the liberation of women than the Catholic Church. They also know that many among them have the gifts and capacity to participate fully in the church. What should their course of action be? Sister Anne Nasimiyu Wasi offers this advice.

> The wholeness of the church of Africa is challenged by several factors, e.g., ethno-centeredness, the love of power and primacy, and the hierarchical structures of the church which undermine the flexibility required by love and justice. Women should continue to challenge the church to a more wholesome, integrative, mutual participation and diversified ministry. They must call attention of all Christians to the service of God's peace and justice to the world.[6]

This is an enormous burden and responsibility to lay upon the backs of Ugandan women, who are already carrying heavy social, political and cultural burdens. Now, when the government is beginning to help them shift their heavy load, they will have more energy to devote to challenging the institutional church to lift the burden of guilt, inferiority and unworthiness it has forced women to bear for so long.

Facing the reality of their situation, Ugandan women spoke to what they felt they must do to awaken the church to the rich potential of women waiting to be called into action.

> We must call the church to train more lay leaders, especially women, to go out and preach to the people.

> We need to begin to educate village women to an awareness of who they are.

> We should encourage young girls to go for theological training and encourage the boys to accept them.

> We need to encourage one another in the realization that we as women are capable of ministering equally or better than men.

> Let us lend supportive hands to one another and help one another arise. For Africa will not arise unless its women-folk, the mothers and bearers of life, arise. What an awesome thought! What a heavy responsibility on our part! May God give us the will to arise and the desire

genuinely to help one another and the whole continent to arise.[7]

Listening to the words of Ugandan women, it is not hard to envision what the fulfillment of their dream for full participation in the church could be:

> Women will go out among the oppressed,
> preach a word of freedom,
> break the bread of justice,
> pour the tears of all the poor
> into their blessing cup and cry:
> We are your chosen people,
> we are a holy nation,
> we are a royal priesthood,
> we are a cherished gender.[8]

8

SET US FREE!

Brazilian women cry out

Liberate us, Free Spirit,
from all that holds us captive within us.
Call us into freedom:
freedom from systems that do not include us;
freedom from structures that do not support us;
freedom from rules that exist to deny us;
freedom from people who refuse to affirm us;
freedom from guilt around and within us;
freedom from fear and its power to deter us.[1]

Brazilian women are becoming more and more aware of their own value as persons and their need to support one another in their struggle for freedom from oppression of all kinds. As indicated earlier, they are the first to admit they have been born into a *machismo* society. Women are brought up to think they are inferior while men are taught from childhood to believe they are superior. To obtain freedom from this oppression, Brazilian women will have to think of themselves as equals. Until recently, most viewed their lives of washing, ironing, cooking and caring for the children as solely their role, never even imagining their husbands should take responsibility also. A few, because they have started to earn money and consequently feel more independent, have begun to change their way of thinking.

Unconsciously mothers create a difference between boys and girls. From infancy boys are given every freedom, while girls are severely restricted. One woman observed, "Unless we as parents begin to educate our children differently, there won't be any change in women's oppression." Another expressed the frustration she felt in trying to do just that. When she told her seven-year-old son to treat his sister as an equal, the boy replied, "Did you happen to notice that God is a man?" It unnerved her to think that a seven year old would have such an awareness! This whole mentality of male superiority is reinforced by church teaching that women are to be submissive, not to be angry or enter into conflict with their husbands. A woman catechist who teaches the marriage course revealed with a smile, "I usually jump over that part. I can't be encouraging the men to dominate us, as if 'It's in the Bible!'"

Brazilian women who have become aware of their oppressive status and have begun to do something about it experience many obstacles. "No one worries about women until we start educating ourselves and begin to move forward. Then people start questioning, but this is the way we have to go," observed a woman from Bahia. Catholic women in Brazil can be described in two ways. There are those who are aware of their oppressed situation, but for various reasons cannot move beyond it. They rely on their faith to sustain them in the face of continuous subjugation. There are others whose deep faith urges them to initiate change, to stand up to unjust treatment whether it be in the form of *machismo* or patriarchy. Neither the church nor society seem to know how to relate to these latter.

The women who came together to be interviewed responded to issues flowing from the questionnaire they had answered the previous year. The questions focused on their role in the church and in society. The 140 women represented all ages and economic levels in the country. There were women from the *favelas* of large and small cities, from the periphery of Sao Paulo, from rural areas and modest towns. Women with large and small families, single women and sisters came, along with women who were homemakers and women who worked outside the home. Women of European, Indian and African backgrounds came and all called themselves "*Brasileiras.*"

Some of the themes that permeated their responses were: a new appreciation of the gifts they as women bring to the church, the obstacles women often present to one another, a realization of the need to unify and support each other, an eagerness to bring about change and the need for ministers who share in their reality.

Women interpret equality

When those interviewed were presented with the fact that more than twice as many of the Brazilian women surveyed felt they were treated more equally in the church than in society, their responses ranged from total surprise and contradiction to full agreement.

There were those who said they truly felt they received equal treatment in the church (by "church" they meant their small base community). Because there are very few men who participate in the base communities, the women do not feel threatened, they encourage one another to take part in the celebrations and even to lead the prayers. Most communities have Mass only once in a fortnight or in a month, so women have many opportunities to plan and conduct their own communion services. Both men and women can be readers, sponsors and eucharistic ministers, but since women far outnumber the men, they have many more chances to participate than they would in an ordinary parish setting. However, some women's participation is severely limited because they are illiterate. "If only I could read," said a woman from the *favela*, "I could participate more in the church and understand the Bible. It's not right to envy others, but we are envious, we'd like to get up there and read too."

Even for them, the community is a haven from the male-dominated society in which they work to supplement the family income. They often do not receive encouragement or support from their husbands. Most husbands fully expect their wives to continue the full care of the house and children when they have an outside job. The fact that the men have some responsibility in the home does not occur to them. Women's own words best describe why women feel as they do in the base communities:

In society there is dispute and competition, but in the community people smile and work together. I can share what I think at the deepest level. The society judges by appearances and has many restrictions against women,

125

race, color, age, etc., but in the community we don't feel that, the community judges by who you are.

The community supports each person, welcomes and values you. You have more liberty in the church and they try to live the gospel that everyone is equal. If you have a problem, the community hears you. You learn a lot, and each day you discover God in different ways.

Women contend that they are equal in the base community because of the acceptance and friendship they experience, but it is only a sense of equality among themselves. As soon as men join the community that sense disappears. Many women who feel so little valued in society feel highly appreciated when they are permitted to do something in the community. Therefore, to the degree they are allowed to participate, women perpetuate this illusion of equality. They know well that the small communities of women valuing women are not the real world, and that what they experience is the exception rather than the norm. Nevertheless, they take strength from their community to return to their home or workplace to continue their struggle for equality.

The small base communities of worship are clearly welcoming and affirming places where women perceive they have value. The first real participation of women in the Brazilian church was in these base communities. There is no way of removing women now because they have discovered their way of being church. They are struggling to remain in these communities because they have found a woman's way to pray.

Other women are clearly aware that this so-called "equality" in the roles they are allowed to perform is an equality only among women. They realize that at the decision-making level women don't really participate, it is only the men. Respondents expressed their disbelief of what the others were saying:

There is no sense in saying anything about equality, there isn't any! The only reason women have anything in the church is because they fight for it, not because it's given to them. But to say a woman has a place in the church is wrong, she doesn't!

Several women expressed their feelings of oppression by both clergy and laymen in the church. "If women don't have strength and determination we'll always be stepped on. We'll always be beneath the man's foot." They revealed that even though the majority working in the base communities are women, if one man shows up, he endeavors to dominate the group. He takes over and makes it clear that what he does is better than what the women do. Though the women feel strongly this is not the way it should be, they too often do not have the courage or the skills to challenge this behavior. "There seems to be a law that men don't treat us as equals," observed a young woman from the rural area. She was answered with the wisdom of the old: "Not God's law, but man's law. God treats everyone as equal!"

"Men today don't seek a place in the church, they are already in positions of power, leaving lesser places for women," noted one woman. Parish meetings are an arena in which women feel their opinions are particularly ignored. They take part in the discussions but when decision-making time comes, the men's opinions are respected much more than the women's. A woman from the interior of the country spoke from her own experience of the church:

> Jesus taught equality, but the church isn't practicing it. I feel more and more that I'm stepped on by the church. Those who dominate most are the priests. When the sisters work with us we have a lot more opportunity, everyone is equal.

In spite of the fact that men do not participate with women in the communities and they feel like "widows" in church, women realize the power that men continue to hold over them even in their absence. However, the women believe in the church because they have built it and continue to hold it together. One graphically described women as "tics" because they stick to what they believe. This was illustrated very simply and profoundly by a woman in a small city in the interior of the country:

> My father questioned why we were raised in a church that only has men making decisions. Then he told me that a house has four walls and four corners, three corners are

held up by the woman and one by the man. If a corner collapses, the house does not fall because the woman is holding up the rest. It is the same with the church. If one side falls, the church won't fall. The women are holding it up!

However, what they do not realize is that by holding up the church as they have done for centuries, women are making it easier for their oppressors to continue to exploit them. What they need to do is let it collapse so that women and men together can build it anew. These women are very realistic about the future. They know that things are not going to change for them overnight, but since women have begun to value their contributions, they can see what progress they have made. As one sister said,

I feel that women have always had a place in the church, but they have never had a voice. They are now discovering that they have a voice, that they are capable of speaking, and when they speak, they make a difference!

The power of change

What would Brazilian women do in the church if they had the opportunity to make changes? They answered this question both practically and creatively:

I'd be a priest! I can dream! I would change the way we celebrate. It is still dependent on one person, the priest. I would like to decentralize the power in the church so that power would be service and not the opportunity to repress and make silent. I'd change the mentality of the people. I'd be a minister with great liberty. I'd have a happy church, one that isn't so gloomy.

They discussed how they would also change the mentality of some of the priests and the bishop, who discriminate against women, especially in times of conflict. They spoke of their desire to be accepted by the priests in their service to the church, accepted in the same way they feel the sisters accept them. Others said they would like to be able to minister to the dying and be able to say "God forgives you."

A Brazilian sister from Bahia described her vision of a participating church, where men and women would share ministries and break bread together. "It's so clear," she said, "I don't understand why it can't be that way!" She then elaborated on her belief that changing practices will change structures, by telling how the women in her base community celebrate eucharist:

> Every week a different woman makes the bread we share. We have all parts of the liturgy—readings, petitions, offering, etc. At the time of communion, the woman who made the bread asks the whole community to bless it, and then we share it. I believe this is eucharist!

Many women are in favor of ordination. They feel that since women are always present in the communities, there is no reason at all why they shouldn't be present in the person of the priest. Some went so far as to question why women have to direct themselves to a male pope and a male bishop. "Why not to a woman?" they asked. "Why not both men and women bishops?"

All of the women, from those in rural areas and *favelas* to the university graduates of Sao Paulo, expressed a desire for change in the church. Several from the interior, however, expressed their fear to initiate this change. They pointed out that people, both men and women, find it difficult to accept even a deacon as minister, and women are criticized when they take communion to the sick. Even the sisters are talked about when they perform these ministries. The fear of making mistakes or of being ostracized by their own people was also mentioned as well as the need for more education. Some women still do not see sacramental or liturgical ministry as their role, while others already perceived some rivalry between women for these positions. Women in Brazil as well as women all over the world could benefit by taking to heart the words of Barbel von Wartenberg-Potter,

> I believe that what women have to do first and foremost is to learn to acknowledge one another as full human beings. To achieve this, we have to work at improving our own low self-esteem and the low value placed on women's activities in our religious and cultural life, and to overcome them in ourselves.[2]

A woman from the interior, who stated she was too old to initiate change (she was fifty-five) cautioned the others, "I'm afraid when women get power they could be just like the men. Some women are just as bad as some men!" No one challenged the wisdom of her insight and a few added to her fear by saying: "We could be worse off with a woman priest. It all depends on her style of ministry" and, "If women were ordained it would throw the church into confusion." Another pointed out that the worst thing in the world is the misuse of power, and she warned that if women are ordained, "It can't be just any woman, but women who are conscientious, women who care about the people and will follow through on what they say." In other words, women don't guarantee a better priesthood.

The majority, however, are eager to pursue a new vision of ministry which would provide equal opportunity for both men and women to function as ordained ministers within the church. Women from the *favelas* and the periphery of the city are convinced, as were the early Christians, that ordained women (and men) should come from and minister to the people of their own base community. "Women who are ordained must come from the people and know their problems." Several said they would accept ordination only if they could serve in their own community. Like the people in the early Christian communities, these women hear the call to: "Brothers [and sisters], select from among you . . . men [and women] filled with the spirit and wisdom, whom we shall appoint to this task" (Acts 6:3).

Women of all ages and levels of education cited numerous advantages that would flow from the ordination of women, both for the church as a whole and for them in particular. They feel that women as priests would understand other women, that it would be so much easier for them to confess to a woman. Many said they don't go to confession now because they don't feel they'll be understood. They also feel that women conduct celebrations better than men because they are more sensitive, and that if women were to preside at the liturgy more people would attend. Looking toward a more inclusive church, a woman from the periphery of Sao Paulo noted:

Men are prejudiced against women, but if they saw them at the altar they might change their minds. Celebrations would be more participative because more women and men would come.

Another woman from a small interior town said she felt it essential to help others be more than they are, and ordination would give that opportunity to women. Reference was made to women's qualities of sensitivity, empathy and compassion along with their ability to be bridge-builders, as ways to bring love and unity to a community in their role of priest.

Several women indicated their indifference as to whether the person presiding at the altar was a man or a woman, but they are clearly not indifferent to women having access to the role of priest. "It doesn't make any difference if it's a woman or a man who presides, the important thing is that the community grows!" In their present situation, women do not feel that is happening as it should because the priest is never among them except once or twice a month to offer Mass and then moves off to the next community. What bothers them is that the priests don't seem to know anything about the people's lives because they are disassociated and detached. The women acknowledged that priests have the gift of a wonderful education, which if combined with the lived experience of the people, would be of enormous worth to the church. They could see what growth would come to them if the priest lived among them, supporting and accompanying them as the sisters do. "The priests, the bishop and the pope should put their feet in our shoes!" they said.

Other women, particularly the more educated, are equally eager for the growth of the community. As one sister explained:

The model of community is the Trinity, but we speak about the Trinity as being far away.... In reality, it is woman who creates and generates community, a trinitarian work where no one is greater than the other....There's a relationship of communion even though the persons are different.

This same woman spoke of her impatience for base communities led by ordained women to become accepted in the church. "I don't think we should wait for structural change. I think the practice has to change and then the structure will change."

Brazilian women are anxious to know about other women in the world who, like them, struggle for equality in the church. Women in the *favelas* and the periphery of the cities find it harder to visualize the women in other countries and cultures than the more educated city women because they have no point of reference. However, all of the women were anxious to know things like the following:

> Do women in other countries participate in movements?
> What is their role in the church?
> Have they won any struggles for equality?
> Do they organize into basic Christian communities?
> Do they have the same problems as we do?
> Do other women have freedom?

They are not sure whether women in other countries have a harder or an easier time. They also want to know what barriers other women have in their struggle, and what are the hardest things they face in their effort to achieve equality. Respondents felt that if women of other countries succeeded, they might use the same model or techniques to achieve equality themselves.

They feel that faith is the common bond among women struggling for equality around the world, along with courage and a certain tenacity. A woman in the *favela* put it clearly, "It's because of the struggle of women that we get anything. Women don't give up. If we unite, a lot of people participate. Because of our example other women get courage." Another, a teacher from the rural area, observed, "If women were allowed to celebrate here in our community, can you imagine how all the women of the world would be so proud of us?"

They assumed that women in the First World were equally eager to learn about them and their efforts. The unfortunate fact is that often this is not so:

> I regret that in the Western women's world there is such an absence of dialogue with sisters around the world about these questions. We are stewing too much in our own juice. . . . We appear to enrich the inner fire of our own

soul and faith at the expense of discerning what is going on in the world. It grieves me to hear women say: "Don't bother me with the Third World, I need to find myself."[3]

Women in Brazil were also able to sit back and look at their own growth and how their awareness of women's value as ministers in the church had been heightened. Several pointed out that when they had filled out the questionnaire the previous year, they had either never thought about women being priests, or were against the idea altogether. Today they see no obstacle to the ordination of women and even say, "Yes, why not!"

These women are discovering their own value. What they do not realize is the many gifts they possess. Women are also beginning to see that there are many among them who need to be awakened. Perhaps the question they need to address is one posed by a simple illiterate woman from the interior named Regina, who makes her living sweeping streets: "The real question is, do women have the same rights as men? If a man has the right to preside, why not a woman? A human being is a human being, man or woman, it doesn't matter." How can the church answer this woman's question with anything but yes in light of the gospel?

Brazilian women and all who are oppressed around the world continue to have hope in Jesus' message of equality and call on one another to channel their energy toward securing their freedom.

Freedom for freeing women to be;
freedom for setting all people free;
freedom for finding the best way to pray
and for coming to God in our own unique way;
freedom for making courageous decisions
to live by the justice the Spirit envisions;
freedom for assuring the climate is free
for you to be you
and for me to be me.
Come, Spirit of Freedom.
Come, set us free.[4]

*"The woman who made the bread
asks the whole community to bless it, and then we share it.
I believe this is eucharist!"*

—*a Brazilian woman*

Part 3

WOMEN CLAIMING THEIR RIGHTFUL PLACE IN THE CHURCH

9

WEAVING WOMEN'S VISIONS

A tapestry of hope

[We are] women weavers
Pulling all the threads
Weaving the names of women
Voices in [our] heads.
[We] shuttle out their teardrops
And [we] latchloop all their cries
As [we] entwine the pain of struggle
Colored patterns tell [us] why.[1]

Certain patterns emerge from the maze of responses and interviews of the over 1260 women on four continents who voiced their pain and suffering along with their prophetic insights regarding their place in society and their invisibleness in the church. What these women have in common is "the experience of living in the mud of marginalization which all women share in one form or another."[2]

If the voices of women are to be believed, society's evaluation of them is clearly negative, if indeed, there is a social valuation at all. Ancient proverbs and local sayings from around the world, along with those previously quoted, lead to the confirmation of this belief. In Asia there is a saying: "Women and soil both improve with beating." The Chinese are even more explicit: "A wife married is like a pony bought; I'll ride her and whip her as I like." African women are equally devalued: "Does your wife work? No, she just stays at home." In Russia, similar to Bangladesh, women are seen as the shadows of men: "I thought I saw two people but it was only a man and his wife." Even though most of these proverbs have their roots in ancient civilizations and their expression in developing countries, women in North America have similar though often unspoken proverbs of their own, e.g., "Better to have a husband who is unfaithful than no husband at all."

In a world that has seldom valued women or their contributions to society, it is no wonder that so many women find it difficult to value themselves or one another. Demographics had no significant effect on how the women in Brazil, Bangladesh, Uganda and the United States felt about society's treatment of them. Whether educated or illiterate, from cities or rural areas, rich or poor, married, single or divorced they communicated their experiences of oppression in ways that were similar while still distinctive. Women most unwilling to speak openly about their distress were the wealthy, though many revealed their feelings in writing as well as their eyes and facial expressions in the oral interviews. Perhaps these women feared public disclosure would result in the loss of their status and identity. For others, acknowledging their own vulnerability was too painful to vocalize.

As might be expected, women in the United States were highest, 89%, in their belief that they are equal to men, followed by 83% in Brazil, 70% in Bangladesh, and 61% in Uganda. However, responses across all four countries were considerably lower when the same women were asked if they felt they were treated as equals in society. Thirty-one percent of Bangladeshi women, 29% of Brazilian women, 22% of the U.S. respondents and only 5% of Ugandan women said they felt they were treated as equals. In order to understand these findings, the level of awareness, the lived experience and the degree of expectation on the part of the women responding must be considered.

Nameless ones

One of the universal prevailing cultural practices that contributes to women's sense of their own insignificance is namelessness. They are some man's daughter, wife or mother with varying degrees of ownership their entire life. Though not specifically mentioned by U.S. women, their nameless situation is graphically described by one of their own.

Traditionally, a woman's life was not her own: she belonged first to daddy and then to husband. Indeed, she was raised with the expectation that she would be literally—body and soul—somebody else's. Today, women are claiming their lives. We still choose love and intimate relationship, but not as reasons for being. We can no longer live through others.[3]

Only recently in the United States have women begun the practice of refusing to take their husband's name when they marry. They struggle to maintain their own hard won identity and risk ridicule in society, often from other women. Rosemary Radford Ruether states women's dilemma well. "The woman who tries to break out of the female sphere into the masculine finds not only psychic conditioning and social attitudes, but the structure of social reality itself ranged against her."[4]

Many women in developing countries have also expressed a desire to be "called by their own name." However, they are most often powerless to take this basic step toward self-identity. Family and traditional cultural pressures, to say nothing of fear, prevent them from exposing themselves to the ridicule and ostracization that would follow such a move.

Peace at any price

The "peace at any price" mode of behavior is another worldwide ploy women use with their husbands, employers or any male authority figure. Many women who have a sense of their own strengths and gifts continue to defer to men by portraying a submissive position, in order to keep peace in the family or workplace. Bangladeshi, Brazilian and Ugandan women along with many U.S. women spoke of getting their husband's permission or letting him think it was "his idea" to do things or go places in order to keep peace. Abuse, whether physical, mental or emotional, is most often the result if these women do not invoke this tactic. Whether women believe in the Bengali proverb or not, those who seek peace at any price find their heaven "under the foot of their husbands."

In countries where women are veiled and must walk a few steps behind their husbands, where they are not permitted to speak when men are present, and where they are valued only in the kitchen or in bed, it is not hard to see the reality of the proverb: "There are no women in these countries, only men and their shadows." But in the United States, where women go bare headed, walk with their husbands, speak in their presence, and are even sometimes valued for their gifts, it is paradoxical that the former First Lady Barbara Bush felt that the country wanted her to appear as a "happy shadow."

Abigail Adams, wife of the second president of the United States, reacted strongly against this concept. She wrote in a letter to her husband John, "While you are proclaiming peace and good will to men, emancipating all nations, you insist upon retaining an absolute power over wives." Such behavior might be expected when the United States was young, but after two hundred years women today might well wonder whether things will ever change.

First Ladies have always drawn criticism. In 1992, as Hillary Rodham Clinton emerged as a First Lady with an independent professional identity, she was a lightning rod for the national ambivalence about the role of women today. Her mere presence reflected the fundamental questions that continue to dog women in our society: Should women have careers? Should they have really good careers, ones even better than their husbands? Should they have them only if they also can do all the housework? Should they voice their opinions, even if doing so might overshadow their mate? Or, should they just keep their place?[5] The sad truth is that in the United States today, many women's best hope for advancement is still to "hitch their wagons to their husbands' stars."

Women belonging to yet a different age, an age when girls were naively taught they could be anything they chose, believed it and have repeatedly encountered the corporate glass ceiling. In every country as soon as young girls reach maturity they experience a reality that challenges their belief in themselves. It is not only in Bangladesh that "the girl-child's fate is forever entwined in her gender."

Education remains the critical tool that gives women the capacity and the ability to insist on their right to participate in society on an equal basis. Most countries have laws providing equal access to education for both boys and girls, but many do not enforce them. This is evidenced by the high rate of illiteracy for girls compared to boys. Even in developed countries, higher education is provided for boys over girls when finances or family tradition are at stake. Women continue to be offered second-hand opportunities simply because they are women. Here too, there is universal application for the Bengali proverb "Educating your daughter is like watering another man's fields."

> At the 1985 U.N. conference in Nairobi, Kenya that closed the decade on women, over thirteen thousand women from all nations of the world expressed their objection to the situation of oppression in song. "We are the world, we are the women. We are the ones who do two-thirds of the world's work, earn ten percent of the world's income, and own less than one percent of the world's assets."[6]

It will take many years before women around the world become fully aware of the sufferings of their sisters in other countries. While women in developing countries are eager and anxious to learn more about women's struggles in the First World, sad to say, the reverse is not always true. A sister in the United States regretfully made the following observation in regard to her own religious community, "We are a collective so engrossed in our own itinerary both spiritually and personally, that we can't see the forest for the trees."

> Perhaps when the day comes that black and white women, poor and middle-class women are able to share their stories—and through that sharing to discover the painful contradictions of women's existence in a patriarchal, competitive and profit-orientated society—then, perhaps, there can be a reconciliation between Sarah the wife and Hagar the concubine.[7]

What makes it even more difficult for women to believe in themselves is the church's continued reiteration of society's devaluation of them, which somehow puts God's stamp of approval on their second-class membership in the human race. As Regina Coll, C.S.J., illustrates:

A search through the catalogue of saints reveals that even when women were canonized they were defined by their biology. Besides martyrs the vast majority of women saints are listed under the categories of virgin, widow and the catch-all "neither virgin nor martyr." . . . Even in scripture women are defined in relationship to a man. Women in the Bible are, ordinarily, someone's wife, mother or whore. This stress on a woman's sexuality has led to a negative and deficient theology of sexuality.[8]

The spirituality of women the world over has been warped by the church's continued emphasis on their sinfulness. It began with Eve's supposed responsibility for the fall of the human race and has continued through history in its emphasis on women's uncleanness and need for purification, and on women as a constant source of temptation. Thomas Aquinas, the great theologian of the Middle Ages, described women as "misbegotten males" necessary to the continuation of the human race, but certainly inferior to males.

A century ago, Elizabeth Cady Stanton, who traveled the world searching for the source of women's subordination and dependence on men found it in the very institution that gives lip service to the equality of all men and women.

What power is it that makes the Hindu woman burn herself on the funeral pyre of her husband? Her religion. What holds the Turkish woman in the harem? Her religion. By what power do Mormons perpetuate their system of polygamy? By their religion. Man, of himself, could not do this; but when he declares, "thus said the Lord," of course he can do it. So long as ministers stand up and tell us that as Christ is head of the church, so is man the head of the woman, how are we to break the chains which have held women down through the ages?[9]

Today, women in Bangladesh, Uganda and Brazil speak of learning, not from the priest, but from the sisters, that they can indeed claim their rights to be readers and eucharistic ministers. "Before," said one Bengali woman, "we were taught that we were unclean and could not go near the altar in the church." The list of devaluations of women is long and culminates in this very decade in which women have been told by the church that they cannot be ordained because they do not image Christ. Women have to wonder just who it is they do image and why they are baptized into a church that continues to devalue them.

Is it any wonder that two thousand years of negative teaching has had a permanent effect on the lives of so many women? "One of the female sins we are guilty of is that we do not really believe that we are God's image, we are only a kind of 'after thought' on the part of the creator."[10] It does not take the wisdom of Solomon to determine where the guilt of this sin lies.

In spite of the heavy burden of history, many women today, enlightened by the Spirit, seek to strengthen their self-image by preparing themselves in both scripture and theology for ministries they feel called to perform. The door to seminaries and theology schools in both Bangladesh and Uganda, however, is labeled "Men Only," strong evidence of how the church in those nations values women's contributions.

In Brazil, as one woman religious remarked, "Our church is going backwards. Up until now women could be admitted to theology schools, but now the door is closed." Is it because Brazilian women theologians are beginning to call the church to conscience, to practice what it preaches about equality, that it is exhibiting such reactionary behavior?

Women in the United States are able to attend theology schools in great numbers and receive Master of Divinity degrees equally with men in universities, but not in seminaries. Their self-image is strong and many feel called to priesthood, but at the end of their studies women are relegated to the pews to witness their fellow students' ordinations. They did not have to earn a Master of Divinity to learn that the church has seven sacraments for men but only six for women. What they cannot understand with all of their learning is how the church can continue to preach Paul's words, "There is not male and female; for you are all one in Christ Jesus" (Gal 3:28).

The fundamental equality of men and women that Paul preaches is not proclaimed by most in leadership roles in the church. Examples include: bishops in Bangladesh who feel women deserve to be beaten; bishops in the United States who forbid women and girls to minister on the altar; bishops in Brazil who fear to allow women to continue to study theology; bishops in Uganda who believe women's work is to do things that do not require an intellect. All of these bishops, and the priests who support them, epitomize the oppressive ecclesiastical structures that keep women in the shadows.

In spite of all these clerical efforts, women today are beginning to realize what the message of Jesus was and is for women as they become painfully aware of their oppression in the church.

> Like the woman [in the gospel] who had a hemorrhage, women now are struggling through the indifferent or hostile throng in their efforts to touch the hem of his garment. . . . Having touched that, we are also summoned to proclaim the healing and hope that have come to us, for this is not a special "women's thing" but the essential message of salvation for the human race.[11]

Women with courage are challenging the church today, they are ignoring criticism, and are publicly testifying that God has indeed made women whole persons who will never again withdraw into the silence of the shadows. A woman living on the periphery of Sao Paulo, Brazil, questioned why there were only men in all the top positions in the church. "Priests, bishops and the pope should put their feet in our shoes and they would understand why we should have women priests." von Wartenberg-Potter put the challenge in a different way.

> Feminist theology has unmasked the sexist structures of church language, theology and social policies. It is fundamentally challenging the church to recognize the distortion of the Christian message created by the church's patriarchal socialization, and to reconstruct its social patterns, language and theology to affirm the full humanity of both women and men.[12]

Another indication of the awakening of women is the high percentage of those who believe that Jesus Christ wants women to be treated as equals in the church. Ninety-eight percent of Brazilian women, 97% Bangladeshi, and 96% Ugandan women affirm this fact, while only 88% of women in the United States are in agreement. Why is the U.S. response 8% to 10% lower than that of women in developing countries?

How does their belief of what should be compare with their experience of what is? Fixing flowers and caring for altar linens are ministries relegated to women in Uganda and Bangladesh, hardly comparable to serving at the altar or chairing the parish council, roles reserved to men and boys. Animating and leading a basic Christian community are roles women in Brazil often perform, but when a man appears "he steps on all the women." Sharing a reflection after holy communion can be done by a woman in the United States, but to give a homily and break open the word of God can only be done by an ordained minister who at this moment in time must also be male. Women feel that the church categorizes them variously as: children, tokens, slaves, temptresses, cheap labor, silent participants, obedient and sub-missive servants, but never as equals or superiors.

Women are protesting against an incomplete, one-sided church and are rising up as the slaves did in the last century against injustices of every sort. The slaves were freed, not because slavery was a demeaning, degrading and inhuman institution, but rather to save the union. If the unity of the church is to be preserved, women must also be given freedom from oppression. Now is the acceptable time for the liberation of women. "Now is the day of salvation" (2 Cor 6:2). The question must be asked of those who represent Jesus in today's church, "How long will the sin of oppression continue to hang over half of the human race?" Elisabeth Schussler Fiorenza has one suggestion:

> The Christian churches will only overcome their oppres-sive patriarchal traditions and their present sexist theologies and praxis if the very basis of these theologies and praxis is changed. If women were admitted to full leadership in church and theology, the need would no longer exist to affirm theologically the maleness of God and Christ and to suppress the Spirit who moves women to full participation in the Christian church and ministry.[13]

The Spirit is indeed blowing through the ranks of Catholic women everywhere. They are joining their voices in a cry for full participation in the church. Even though there are varied degrees of meaning regarding full participation for women, in Third World countries 81% indicated that they would like more opportunity to take part in the church. An average of 83% believe they should have equal decision-making power, and 77% affirm equal access to leadership positions with men should be theirs. Sixty-seven percent of the women were strong in their desire to preach homilies, adding in every country, "women could preach even better than men." An average of 52% would like to see women ordained deacon or priest. The universal question is, "If our sisters in other churches can be ordained, why not us?"

An even stronger universal concern that women voiced was not for themselves but for those of the next generation. "We want a church for our daughters," was the cry from U.S. women. "It may be too late for me but surely not for my daughter," observed a Ugandan woman. A Bangladeshi woman wisely stated "If we begin, we can slowly, slowly accomplish this for those who come after us." In Brazil where women are already doing so much in the base communities, they look to their daughters to do even more. However, for women in the towns, the desire is even stronger. "We go to Mass week after week and it's the same old thing, the priest does his thing, boring! You put a woman in their in the future and we would be radiant! We'd be so proud!" There is hope mixed with despair as women look at the church today and ask, "What's for our daughters?"

Rosemary Haughton reminds us that in the beginning it was not so, as she points an accusing finger at the patriarchal church.

> When we get in touch with what happened to those women who followed Jesus in his earthly lifetime and later, we find that the attitude of Jesus to women, and their response to it, is at the heart of his promise of liberation for the whole creation. Because of the refusal of the Christian church to follow him in this, Jesus' mission has not been carried out, except here and there in patches.[14]

Well over half of the women surveyed indicated their awareness of these patches when they answered no to the question, "Do you believe the message of Jesus regarding equality for women is practiced in the church today?" They can also point to numerous areas of church life which are thin and worn, where the inclusion of women would strengthen the fabric of the church's liberating message.

Fear of women

Catholics today, particularly in the United States, are accused of "supermarket spirituality," picking and choosing those aspects of the church's teaching that please them and discarding the others. Has not the hierarchical church done the same for centuries in excluding women from its language, its liturgy, its leadership and its ministry? Is this exclusion simply because women do not please the clergy and hierarchy or is it because the hierarchy and clergy simply fear women? How many times in the New Testament do we hear Jesus say, "Fear not!" How many stories are told of those who have overcome their fear to reach out to him? The blind Bartimaeus sitting by the roadside is certainly one example. He overcame his fear, threw off his cloak and followed Jesus. If it is fear that is blinding the clergy and hierarchy let them, like Bartimaeus, throw off their mantle of fear and follow Jesus' example in their treatment of women.

Questions and statements relative to this issue came from women everywhere. A Ugandan woman spoke of the priest who closed down programs for women because they were challenging him about church teachings and practices. "No one in the church worries about women until we start educating ourselves," noted a Brazilian woman who had just been relieved of her position in a parish. A sister in Bangladesh, who was highly educated, described how her parish priest forced her to leave on the pretext that she was too proud. "A priest I was working with," noted a U.S. woman, "felt insecure because more people were coming to hear me than him."

As I have already noted, in order to continue to minister even minimally in the church many women employ the "peace at any price" tactic, familiar to both husbands and clergy alike. U.S. women are willing to give up their role of lector, acolyte or eucharistic minister on the days the bishop visits keeping them perpetually on the periphery. Rather than allow altar girls, a priest in an eastern city parish recruited Protestant boys because he did not have enough Catholic boys to serve.

147

A Ugandan woman who works at the diocesan level for women's literacy, self-awareness and self-help struggles to keep a low profile. "I told the bishop I could teach under a tree," she said. She asked for no title or office in order not to threaten the priests and their power base or lose the opportunity to work for women. Women experience great tension between "peace at any price" in order to accomplish a desired good and cooperating in their own oppression.

Women in Bangladesh described what they are forced to do in order to maintain their place on the parish council. "When we tell the truth, how we really think, we are not accepted. If we vote with the men in a meeting, we are accepted, but not if we disagree." Many admitted that they cannot stand up to the social pressure.

Women in a base community in Brazil, who lead their Sunday service each week in a meaningful way, told how they sit back and do nothing when the priest comes for monthly Mass. "He comes in, gives all the orders, says Mass and leaves. He doesn't relate to us nor we to him." Rather than struggle for their part in the celebration, they remain passive.

In their eagerness to minister, women often make the mistake of equating such selective participation with equal participation and do not see it for what it really is—"crumbs from the table." They are too often dancing to the tune of the clergy who "allow" them to minister when it is convenient, when they keep their place and when they do not challenge the status quo. Some are caught up in the "God's will" syndrome and say, "I see changes happening slowly. If it's God's will, more will happen." Others express impatience with this mentality.

> I've become aware of the way things work in other churches. I've glimpsed what we could have so when I hear women say, it will come eventually, I say, "O God, please shake some branches." I'm watching women in other denominations work side by side with men taking leadership roles, being given authority. I say to myself, "Why am I staying in my own church? Why are we on such a different time-line from the Protestants?"

According to one Hispanic woman, the test of real equality in ministry happens when one does

> not ... sit back and accept whatever happens. It's a matter of having the courage to speak the truth. When you speak, you'll be mocked and you'll be categorized. So you speak and you speak and you speak and you become a thorn in somebody else's side. You make people very uncomfortable. That's the role of a Christian, to make people very uncomfortable with their lack of freedom.

To take a position as a disciple of Jesus is to stand spiritually at the foot of the cross open to his message, ready to spread the good news for women, that part of the message of Jesus that has been forgotten through the centuries. Jesus went about his ministry seeking to change the hearts of men and women. He didn't totally succeed, but his message went out to the ends of the earth. Today, women are asking themselves, "How much courage do I have to make this happen?"

> The civil rights movement in the U.S.
> took its heart from one woman
> who would no longer sit
> in the back of the bus,
> who would no longer accept
> her enslavement,
> no longer live with the status quo.
> The status quo is so comfortable
> for us
> so safe, so easy.
> We know the cost of breaking out of that:
> it can be terribly high.
> It can even be death.[15]

If one black woman, Rosa Parks, could act as a catalyst for the Civil Rights Movement, imagine what tens of thousands of women around the world could do to obtain equal rights if they were willing to challenge the institutional church. Throughout church history there have been many "Rosa Parks" who refused to sit mutely in the pews, but did not find the same support. Today, as the consciousness of women is heightened, many more women are rising and encouraging others to claim their rightful place in the church.

If the church is, in fact, seeking to ignore the "problem" of strong western women and looking to developing countries where it is growing, in the hope of dealing with docile, submissive women, it should be prepared for a surprise. Indian lay theologian Astrid Lobo Gajiwala is a prime example.

> The institutional church's patriarchal attitude forces women to question church relevance to their personal, moral and spiritual development. We dislike being controlled, patronized and double-crossed.[16]

The sari-clad theologian from Bombay also urged church leaders to listen to women with respect and care, because women will abandon the official church if its apathy toward their problems does not change. Women such as Gajiwala are speaking out in many countries. They are reminding other women as well of Vatican II's message to the world. The church as the People of God calls all its member—bishops, priests and laity—to perform acts of liberation as Jesus did, deeds that are signs and proof of the presence of God's justice and mercy in the world. These women are now asking, "Where are the signs and proof of the presence of God's justice in the institutional church's treatment of women?"

Women in the First and Third Worlds have experienced suffering in society and in the church. In Paul's words,

> [They] are often troubled, but not crushed; sometimes in doubt, but never in despair; [they have] many enemies, but [they] are never without a friend; and though badly hurt at times, [they] are not destroyed. At all times [they] carry in [their] mortal bodies the death of Jesus, so that his life also may be seen in [them] (2 Cor 4:8-10, *Today's English Version*).

However, as previously stated, African women theologians warn that it is vicarious suffering, freely undertaken, which is salvific—not involuntary victimization. To choose to fast or to give alms is salvific, but to be starved or robbed is victimization. Women are more than willing to give to the church without counting the cost in the spirit of salvific suffering, but when the institutional church oppresses and ignores them, excludes, demeans and diminishes them, women realize they are being victimized.

In 1986, Third World women theologians met in Oaxtepec, Mexico to explore the topic, "Doing Theology from Third World Women's Perspective." The final document issuing from the conference emphasized:

> In all three continents (Asia, Africa and Latin America) women constitute a vital and dynamic force within the church. Our strong faith and numerous services of love keep the church alive, especially among the poor and the marginalized. Yet though we constitute a strong labor force within the heavily institutionalized church, we are powerless and voiceless, and in most churches are excluded from leadership roles and ordained ministries.[17]

The document then sets forth a challenge to Third World women, one which also calls women from North America to stand in solidarity with them in their struggle. "This deplorable condition urgently calls for sustained efforts to discover new ways of being church, of being in the world as the visible presence of God's reign, and of the new creation."

Bishops of the world, including the Bishop of Rome, must hear women's challenge. The U.S. bishops listened to women for almost a decade in an effort to write a pastoral letter on women's concerns. However the bishops failed to approve the fourth draft of that letter at their November, 1992 meeting. The draft is published as a committee report without the teaching authority of the bishops' conference. Bishops in the developing countries have not even begun to listen. The task is far from complete. To fail to listen and respond as Jesus would is to betray his mission.

How will we recognize this new way of being church? Will men become weavers with women to create a tapestry that reveals the full face of God? The institutional church repeatedly depicts God as male, thereby eliminating other concepts. Scripture tells us we are all made in God's image, male and female. Women admitted to all ministries, would add to our concept of God by incorporating the feminine. Women from the Third World observe that "without women's perspective and their contribution to theology, God, Jesus Christ, the Holy Spirit, salvation, church and mission will be only half understood."[18] A woman from Texas spoke of the necessity of the inclusion of women with men in the church in order that it might become whole.

> The whole is not present. We have only half a picture and that makes me very sad. Not until we come together and understand each other, can we see God's face. I think that is the only time we can see God's whole face.

Women from all countries of the world are waiting to weave the tapestry that will reveal the full face of God.

> [We are] the women weavers
> Pulling all the threads
> Weaving the pain of women
> Some now living some now dead.
> And [we] shuttle out their wisdom
> And [we] gather all their grace
> As [we] unravel here before [us]
> This woman-loving lace.[19]

Women are ready with their colored threads and fibers symbolizing their oppression and pain as well as their joy and their hope. Only when men are willing to invite women to join them at the loom can they weave a new tapestry in which all will see the full face of God!

10

LET THERE BE BREAD!

Not just crumbs

And God's sisters
knelt on the earth, planted the seeds
prayed for the rain, sang for the grain
made the harvest, cracked the wheat
pounded the corn, kneaded the dough
kindled the fire, filled the air
with the smell of fresh bread
And there was bread!
And it was good![1]

There is a tension in the universal church today. There is a sense of confusion among both men and women regarding Jesus' treatment of the women of his time and the experience of women in the church today. Scripture clearly demonstrates that Jesus went against the prevailing Jewish customs when he spoke to women in public and included them among his followers.

> Women in Judaism were not recognized as valid witnesses. In honoring the woman at the well as well as the women after the resurrection, Jesus broke through this barrier to motivate women to be his first messengers/witnesses.[2]

If the institutional church had continued to include women as Jesus did, as messengers and preachers, the cries of women for equality today would be unnecessary. The men in Jesus' time not only misunderstood him, but they also could not fully accept his inclusion of women. This is the legacy they passed on to their successors who have held women's rejection in trust even until now. Rosemary Haughton reveals how this came to be.

> Jesus had given these women unprecedented freedom, and the men in the church could not live with this. Their whole cultural identity was threatened by the behavior of the women, and in the end the sheer weight of custom was stronger than the impulse of new life.[3]

Through the centuries, small groups of women have realized their deprivation and exclusion and have struggled without success to regain that original freedom. The majority have passively conformed to what the patriarchal church allowed them to do. Today, many Catholic women are realizing that it is time to bury forever the unspoken proverb they have been giving life to for centuries. "It is better to be a silent member in a church that excludes and demeans you than not to be a member at all."

Catholic women are speaking up, both in the United States and in developing countries. Women's voices are rising in every corner of the world, calling the institutional church to open its mind and heart to Jesus' message of equality for women. They describe clearly and simply what that means:

> to serve and learn how to deepen their faith;
> to use their baptismal gifts to the fullest;
> to be included in the liturgical language of the church;
> to minister sacramentally to the People of God;
> to share as equals in shaping the reign of God;
> to receive official acknowledgment of their call to priesthood.

Women deserve full membership in the church of Jesus Christ. It is so clear that even the most illiterate cannot understand why it can't be that way. The strength of women's voices together with the validity of their arguments make it difficult to understand how the hierarchical church could even consider accepting a stalemate on the role of women in a church that preaches all are created equal.

Unfortunately, until now the church has turned a deaf ear to these basic requests for full participation, forcing women into a tragic double-bind. According to Mary Jo Weaver "whatever choice women make forces them to deny some part of their identity." She describes their dilemma.

> If they stay within the institution they have to repress any consciousness of women's questions (about language, discrimination, opportunities) and embrace a tradition that defines them without consulting them. If they leave, it appears that they have given up on their heritage and denied their Catholicity.[4]

Women are struggling for an identity within a church that both oppresses them and gives them life. The life-giving message of Jesus for all throughout the New Testament is clearly revealed in John 10:10 (*Today's English Version*), "I have come in order that [you] might have life, life in all its fullness." Nowhere in his message do we find Jesus speaking of oppression for either women or men. Even though Jesus lived in a land where women were devalued and oppressed, he consistently defied that culture by repeatedly lifting women up and giving them life.

What today's women cannot understand is that in spite of Jesus' example the church, after two thousand years of preaching the Good News, continues its oppressive treatment of them. We have to ask what excuse the church has for not treating women as Jesus did. In a matter so clearly contrary to the message of the gospel, women see the precise necessity for dialogue, for reconciliation and for affirmative action. They have to question why it is so hard for the hierarchy, most of whom have been schooled in scripture, to understand this.

Women's exclusion is a global issue

It is obvious from the stories women told me that their history of exclusion, oppression and diminishment in the institutional church is far removed from the consciousness of the church hierarchy. As a result, most bishops fail to comprehend the injustice of such actions. The very fact that many among the hierarchy consider women's struggle for full participation to be "a North American problem and one that sensible women do not want," illustrates their distance from women's reality.[5]

Hundreds of women on four continents throughout the pages of this book have spoken of the pain of their exclusion and their unfulfilled hopes for equality. Women's souls are freezing to death in our churches for many reasons, not the least being the denial of the life-giving warmth that would come from receiving the sacrament of the sick or the sacrament of reconciliation from another woman. Men, on the other hand, experience that warmth and comfort daily. In the face of such inequality women are forced to ask the hierarchy how they can presume to call them to be partners in the mystery of redemption? Partners connote equality and there is no basis for such a presumption in the Catholic Church today.

We who remain in the church do so for a number of reasons. These range from those who have never thought of leaving to those who stay because they believe it is their church and no one is going to put them out of it. In between are women who are teetering on the periphery and waiting to see if things are going to change, as well as those struggling with questions central to their whole Catholic identity. How does the hierarchy answer questions like:

Who are we as women in the church?

What is our personal and collective identity?

What ever happened to the message of Jesus for us?

How can the church reconcile women's exclusion from language, ministry and leadership with its teaching on justice?

Women I spoke with on all four continents are demanding answers to these questions. It is obvious that the church cannot expect to be taken seriously by women as long as such flagrant injustices prevail.

Other women the world over are echoing the cry of the psalmist, "How long, O God, will you hide your face from us? How long will you look the other way when we are in need?" (see Ps 13). From the time of Jesus women have been begging for answers to these questions. Jesus responded positively to the women of his time. We have only to think of the Samaritan woman, Mary Magdalene, the woman with the issue of blood, the widow of Naim, the bent-over woman, Martha and Mary and in particular, the Canaanite woman. She exhibited the courage and tenacity so many others have emulated in their struggle for justice throughout the ages. When will today's church give us the same affirmation?

As recently as 1992, while denying women equality of roles in the church, the bishops of the United States ironically acknowledged that "in every age women have led the way by their exemplary efforts to remedy injustice."[6] Is it unreasonable to expect the bishops to follow the lead of women to remedy the injustices the church perpetrates against them, or does a critical interpretation of living the message of Jesus allow for a middle-of-the road response? Alicia Faxon throws down the gauntlet to the hierarchy in *Women and Jesus*. "The revolutionary doctrine of equal status has been proclaimed and practiced by Jesus and is ours to fulfill."[7] Women both within and outside the dominant western culture, are joining their voices in solidarity with this challenge.

Unlike the Canaanite woman, Catholic women today are refusing to pick up the crumbs that fall from the clerical table. For too long they have been the recipients of fragments of power, particles of authority, portions of ministries, splinters, shreds and pieces of membership and participation in a church that consistently takes all they give and gives them only crumbs in return. Is it any wonder they are rising up against such injustices?

Gerda Lerner reminds us that "for nearly four thousand years women have shaped their lives and acted under the umbrella of patriarchy, specifically a form of patriarchy best described as paternalistic dominance."[8] In commenting on the failure of the American bishops to address and respond to women's concerns honestly in the various drafts of the women's pastoral, Bishop Francis Murphy eloquently describes the sins of patriarchal dominance in the church.

> Dominance pervades our church, a dominance that excludes the presence, insights, and experience of women from the "table" where the formulation of the church's doctrine takes place and the exercise of its power is discerned. It likewise excludes women from presiding at the table where the community of faith is fed. This patriarchy

continues to permeate the church and supports a climate that not only robs women of their full personhood, but also encourages men to be domineering, aggressive, and selfish.[9]

Patriarchy has not only dominated, excluded and robbed women, but it has also exemplified for them that such behavior is rewarded in the church. There are many depressing stories of women dominating, suppressing, and demeaning other women for their own selfish gains, indicating how deeply the two-edged sword of patriarchy has permeated our lives.

The hierarchy speaks of women's gifts as being different but complementary to those of men. They concentrate on the differences between men and women and in doing so are blinded to what makes them one, their baptism into Christ.

What the institutional church needs, says Caroline Julia Bartlett, is to be mothered as well as fathered.

Until the creeds are humanized, which were formulated by the early "church fathers" and by our Puritan forefathers; until the lost balance of religion is restored by the restoration of the woman's element to the mutilated human and the mutilated divine; until motherhood as well as the fatherhood of God is recognized by this world of self-made half-orphans; until these things be, the supreme call to the ministry that vibrates through the world today is to womanhood to give herself to the service of unifying and uplifting humanity, and bringing it up to the true knowledge and glad service of our Father and Mother God.[10]

Women in Brazil, Bangladesh and Uganda along with hundreds in the United States told me that they are tired of weeping, of waiting, of being silenced and ignored. They are weary of giving so much and receiving so little in return. If the bishops cannot respond out of a sense of justice, they may be forced to do so for the sake of peace, because these women will not be quiet.

Like their Canaanite predecessor, women will continue to press their demands for justice until the institutional church acknowledges their baptismal right to stand at the altar table as equal partners in the breaking of the bread.

The disciples asked Jesus to send the Canaanite woman away because she was troubling them with her begging and pleading. Today's Catholic women will not go away. On the contrary they have become increasingly present in this post Vatican II era. Eighty-five percent of new parish ministers in the U.S. church are women. If in fact they did go away, "the pastoral activity of the Catholic Church would grind to an almost complete halt."[11]

If that were to happen, if women in every country would stage a walkout and leave the church completely to men, I believe the women would suffer the least because for so many, their spiritual nourishment comes from sources outside the institutional church where they feel valued. Women described to me the numerous ways they find God as they come together to pray, share the scripture and break bread. "What a difference it makes when women preside, they make everyone feel a part of the meal." Women feel included in ways currently not possible in the institutional church. These are "sacramental moments" and God is certainly present among them.

Among these women are prophets who, in the tradition of the prophets, envision a church that embraces them as full sacramental ministers and challenges the institution to accept that vision. They imagine a future in which women, who comprise the majority of church-goers and church-doers, see themselves as full partners in the mystery of redemption. These women prophets are not confined to North America and Europe. They are also rising up in increasing numbers in Asia, Africa and Latin America, continents where, according to Swiss missiologist Walbert Buhlmann, O.F.M. Cap., more than 70% of the Catholics of the world will be living by the year 2000.[12]

Rosemary Haughton asserts that without the vision of these women prophets, "we remain stuck, which is why revolutions are the result not simply of intolerable conditions, but of intolerable conditions plus a voice that cries out that something else is imaginable and possible."[13] As Haughton indicates, feminist prophesy requires imagination to a profound degree.

Women prophets speak of what is imaginable and possible in the church. Scripture tells us that God poured out the Spirit on both menservants and maidservants of old, yet women prophets of today must ceaselessly defend themselves against the denunciations of their male counterparts. Does the institutional church in its continuous attempt to silence women's prophetic voices do so because it fears the truth of what women predict?

When I met the second time with the women in Bangladesh, Uganda and Brazil I sensed a new vitality among them. There was an energy arising from the awareness that they are not alone in their struggle, that there are others who share their vision of equality and justice for women in the church. When I spoke about the vision of women in developing countries with women in the United States, many were surprised to learn that in spite of their enormous social problems, these women were as concerned about their identity and role in the church as are First World women.

How is it that women in such disparate cultures, races and language groups, thousands of miles apart on four different continents could have identical questions about their church and envision similar solutions? Their questions along with their proposed solutions seek to remedy injustice and are grounded in the gospel. It behooves the institutional church to pay attention because it can no longer use the argument that this is a North American problem, nor can they claim it to be a women's problem. Rather, this is the problem of the hierarchy of the universal church and it will not go away.

One group of women responsible for this rising chorus of women's voices from around the world is Catholic sisters, who minister as both teachers and pastoral agents. The women in almost every group I interviewed, particularly in the developing countries, credited the sisters with the responsibility for raising their awareness to their own dignity as women with equal rights in society and in the church.

These Catholic sisters have done the most to renew the church since Vatican II. Many among them are strong in their feminist beliefs and are perceived by some members of the hierarchy, in spite of their diminishing numbers, as posing a threat to the established order. However, the seeds have already been planted in the formation programs these sisters are directing in developing countries. Vocations are flourishing and young Asian, African and Latin American sisters are even now preaching and teaching Jesus' message of equality for women in the church.

At the "Call to Action" workshop in Chicago in November, 1991, theologian Terry Dosh indicated his belief that Rome had decided to wait and let these communities of sisters die out rather than fight such strong women. Contrary to this belief, the very next year the Vatican approved a second organization separate from L.C.W.R., the official Leadership Conference of Women Religious. "The creation of a separate organization establishes a new and troublesome precedent," said L.C.W.R. leaders, "especially at a time when the church is attempting to unify people while ministering in a pluralistic society."[14] This division threatens the unity among women religious of the United States that L.C.W.R. has strived to achieve since 1956.

A significant part of the message of renewal from Vatican II that many Catholic sisters have internalized is the recognition of the laity as "People of God," called to be apostles and ministers. Because we belong to the laity ourselves we have come to walk hand in hand in ministry, particularly with women the world over. My experience has given me the enriching opportunity to hear the voices of women speak to their conviction that the status of women in the church and the quality of relationships between men and women are critical to our being a community of integrity, a credible sign of justice and peace in our world. Such a community would be characterized by equality between women and men; by the absence of patterns of subordination and domination; and by the recognition that we are inter-dependent.

The synergism of women awakening

The awakening of women, their growing numbers, their desire for more education and their conviction of the truth of their vision are producing a synergism that will enable women to rise, to demand answers to their questions and to begin to hold the patriarchal church accountable. An overwhelming 94% of the women polled in my research indicated their belief that Jesus Christ wants women to be treated equally in the church. Is it possible or even probable that so many women in so many different countries are wrong? Whatever happened to *sensus fidelium*, to the church's acceptance of the faith of its people?

Several American bishops are currently speaking to the necessity of continuing dialogue on this issue. One considers it to be "as important as the issue Paul raised with Peter; namely, the admission of Gentiles into Christianity. Women's calls, as well as men's" he said, "should be tested. Justice demands it. The pastoral needs of the church require it."[15]

Catholic women realize that they are challenging centuries of tradition in the church and that this is very serious indeed. They know how difficult change is for so many people. Yet, as is stated so well in the Pastoral Constitution on the Church in the Modern World,

> The church has always had the duty of scrutinizing the signs of the times and of interpreting them in the light of the gospel. Thus in language intelligible to each generation, she can respond to the perennial questions which are asked about this present life and the life to come, and about the relationship of the one to the other.[16]

Thirty years ago John XXIII recognized the rising consciousness of women as one of the signs of our times. I feel certain that if he were here today, he would interpret this sign of our times, and respond to this perennial question with: "Let the women be there. Let the women be all they can be. Let the women be there."

For centuries women and men have prayed the words that Jesus taught us with great faith and expectation, "Give us today our daily bread." Thus far, it is men who have received the fullness of that bread. In order to sustain themselves, women continue to collect their daily crumbs. Richard McBrien suggests a strategy for their survival: "Live in the present as if it were already the future. Women should act now as if their baptismal dignity and ministerial equality were already acknowledged."[17] Women should take pastoral initiatives and assume leadership roles consistent with their gifts and the call of their faith-communities. "Doing the will of God," he observes, "often requires courage, sometimes even a form of martyrdom. So does living in the present as if the future were already here."

Doing the will of God has a multitude of meanings for women when it comes to their role in the church. For some, it still means maintaining silence, preserving the peace and permitting men and women to do what they have always done. In other words, "If God wants things to change, they will." The question for these women persists, "Is this really what God intends, or what men want women to believe?"

Doing the will of God for the growing multitude of women the world over means something entirely different. For them it means speaking the truth, disturbing the peace, claiming our equal place in the church's ministry and challenging the institutional church to live the true message of the gospel. This new awareness, like yeast, is causing women around the world to rise up and claim their future.

What a new moment it would be for the institutional church and for the People of God if the bishops of the world would engage honestly in a profound reconsideration of soul in addressing the concerns of women in the church.

To paraphrase the author of Ecclesiastes, there is a time for everything:

A time for weeping and a time for rejoicing;
A time for keeping silence and a time for speaking;
A time for sitting in the pews and a time for preaching;
A time for waiting and a time for acting;
A time for submitting and a time for rising up.

Women throughout the centuries have had more than enough time to weep, to keep silence, to wait, to submit, and to sit in the pews. Today, thousands of women the world over feel that time is over and now is the time for them to rejoice, to speak up, to act, to preach, to rise up and claim their rightful place in the church.

The time is now. The women are rising and the church will be blessed!

POSTSCRIPT

As I come to the moment of sending this book to the publisher, I realize that I have not just completed a gigantic research project and can now return to my normal life of teaching and administration. Instead, I have been propelled into a lifelong ministry of raising the world's awareness to the valuable contributions women can make, want to make and feel called to make to a church which denies and neglects them.

To facilitate this ministry an endowment has been established entitled:

The Sister Francis B. O'Connor, C.S.C., Endowment for Ongoing Research and Scholarships to Promote Women's Equality in the Church

The specific purpose of the endowment is to bring women to an awareness of the injustices of patriarchy and instill in them a sense of their own worth, thereby enabling them to contribute their gifts to the church equally with men.

The two main objectives include: the distribution and translation of this book and its accompanying video *Crumbs From the Table* (also available from Ave Maria Press) in Bangladesh, Brazil, Uganda and the United States, and the ongoing scriptural and theological education of women in developing countries and the U.S.A. All royalties from the sale of this book will be applied to the endowment. Contributions to this ministry can be made to:

The Sister Francis B. O'Connor, C.S.C., Endowment
c/o Sisters of the Holy Cross
Saint Mary's
Notre Dame, IN 46556

APPENDIX A

Catholic Women Survey

The letter and survey instrument were adapted and translated for Bangladesh, Brazil and Uganda. The following is the version used in the United States.

University of Notre Dame, Notre Dame, IN, USA 46556   Kellogg **INSTITUTE**

Dear Respondent,

The enclosed questionnaire is part of a research project entitled: "Contemporary Women's Response in the Roman Catholic Church: An International Inquiry."

The proposed study will be unique in that it will consider the ways in which Catholic women are interacting with, or leaving the institutional church. It will address the fundamental question, "What choices are Catholic women making in order to achieve full participation in the church?"

This research is being conducted jointly by and for lay and religious women in four countries of the world: the United States, Brazil, Bangladesh and Uganda. It is an effort to ascertain what women in these countries are doing in their church, and what they would like to do. The research will also seek to discover the efforts women are making to become recognized and accepted as equal persons in the institutional church.

You have been selected from among the Catholic Women in the United States to receive a questionnaire. Everything on this questionnaire will be treated as confidential. The time required for completion is approximately 30 to 45 minutes. In order for our results to be representative it is very important that those who receive a survey fill it out and return it.

The results of the total study will be published in written and video form and will be available for parish and diocesan study groups.

Thank you for your time and consideration.

Sister Francis B. O'Connor, C.S.C.
Guest Scholar, Kellogg Institute
University of Notre Dame

The Helen Kellogg Institute for International Studies

219/239-6580   Fax: 219/239-6717

CATHOLIC WOMEN SURVEY — U.S.A.

(Please circle the number or fill in the blank with the answer that best represents your response.)

1. Age

    1   UNDER 20
    2   20 - 29
    3   30 - 39
    4   40 - 49
    5   50 - 59
    6   60 - 69
    7   OVER 69

2. A. Where do you live?

    City _____ State _____

    B. What is your Racial/Ethnic
       background?

    _____

3. Which best describes the area in which
   you live?

    1   RURAL AREA
    2   TOWN UNDER 10,000 POPULATION
    3   TOWN OF 10,000 - 24,999
    4   TOWN OF 25,000 - 99,999
    5   CITY OF 100,000 - 499 999
    6   CITY OF OVER 500,000

4. Are you presently

    YES NO
    1   2   a. WORKING
    1   2   b. RETIRED
    1   2   c. SEEKING EMPLOYMENT
    1   2   d. HOMEMAKER
    1   2   e. OTHER (please specify)

    _____

5. Current Occupation

    1   PROFESSIONAL
         (doctor, nurse, lawyer, CPA, etc.)
    2   MANAGEMENT/ADMINISTRATOR
    3   OFFICE WORKER
    4   TEACHER
    5   SALES
    6   STUDENT
    7   SERVICE/MAINTENANCE
    8   OWN BUSINESS
    9   OTHER (specify): _____

6. If you are employed, how many hours per week do you work?   _ _ hours

7. In which of the income groups below was your total income for 1989 before taxes?
   If you are married, please indicate family income figure.
   (Circle the appropriate number.)

    1   LESS THAN $12,000   6 $35,000 to $49,999
    2    $12,000 TO $14,999   7 $50,000 to $74,999
    3    $15,000 TO $19,999   8 $75,000 to $99,999
    4    $20,000 TO $24,999   9 $100,000 AND ABOVE
    5    $25,000 TO $34,999

8. Please circle the highest level of education you have completed.
   (Circle the appropriate number.)

    1   GRADE SCHOOL   6   SOME GRADUATE WORK
    2   SOME HIGH SCHOOL   7   A GRADUATE DEGREE
    3   COMPLETED HIGH SCHOOL   (specify degree and major)
    4   SOME COLLEGE
    5   COMPLETED COLLEGE   _____
         (specify major) _____

9. Which type of School did you attend for the majority of your education?

    a. CATHOLIC   b. PUBLIC

10. Indicate the categories of continuing education programs in which you have participated.

YES	NO			YES	NO		
1	2	a.	RELIGION	1	2	f.	SOCIAL WORK
1	2	b.	BUSINESS	1	2	g.	LAW
1	2	c.	SCIENCE	1	2	h.	COMPUTER SCIENCE
1	2	d.	ARTS/LETTERS	1	2	i.	OTHER (specify) _____
1	2	e.	MEDICINE/NURSING				

11. Are you presently

    1 MARRIED   4 NEVER MARRIED
    2 DIVORCED   5 WIDOWED
    3 SEPARATED

	YES	NO	N/A
12. In your first marriage, were you married by a Catholic priest?	1	2	3
13. If married more than once, was your present marriage witnessed by a Catholic Priest?	1	2	3
14. Have you ever sought an annulment?	1	2	
15. Was an annulment granted?	1	2	
16. How many children do you have?........................ _____ CHILDREN			
17. Were your children Baptized?	1	2	3

	YES	NO	SOMETIMES	NEVER
18. Do/Did your children attend CCD or Catholic Schools?	1	2	3	4

	YES	NO
19. Are you currently a woman religious?	1	2

IF YES, HOW MANY YEARS _ _ years   CONGREGATION _____

	YES	NO
20. Were you previously a woman religious?	1	2

IF YES, HOW MANY YEARS _ _ years   CONGREGATION _____

	YES	NO
21. Are you, or have you ever been, a member of a Third Order or Associate Group of a religious community?	1	2

IF YES, WHICH ONE _____

LIKE BREAD, THEIR VOICES RISE!

	YES	NO

22. What Catholic newspapers or periodicals do you read?

		YES	NO
a.	NATIONAL CATHOLIC REPORTER	1	2
b.	YOUR DIOCESAN PAPER	1	2
c.	THE CATHOLIC REGISTER	1	2
d.	AMERICA	1	2
e.	CATHOLIC DIGEST	1	2
f.	OUR SUNDAY VISITOR	1	2
g.	THE WANDERER	1	2
h.	OTHER (specify)	1	2

23. Politically, which **one** of the following categories best describes you? (Circle the appropriate number.)

    1 A STRONG REPUBLICAN
    2 A MODERATE REPUBLICAN
    3 INDEPENDENT LEANING TOWARD REPUBLICAN
    4 INDEPENDENT
    5 INDEPENDENT LEANING TOWARD DEMOCRAT
    6 A MODERATE DEMOCRAT
    7 A STRONG DEMOCRAT
    8 INDIFFERENT

	YES	NO
24. Are you a registered voter?	1	2
25. Are you a baptized Catholic?	1	2
26. Were you a member of another religion before you were received into the Catholic Church?	1	2

27. If YES, what religion were you before and why did you become a Catholic?

	YES	NO	SOMETIMES
28. Do you receive the sacrament of Reconciliation?	1	2	3
29. Do you receive the Eucharist?	1	2	3
30. Do you consider yourself a Catholic?	1	2	3

(If answering YES to the above question, SKIP to Question #34.)

31. When and why did you leave the Catholic Church? _____

    Why? _____

APPENDIX A

	YES	NO

32. Do you belong to another religion? 1   2

    Please indicate your religion: _____

33. What does your present religious practice provide for you that the Catholic Faith did not?

    _____

    _____

34. Do you consider yourself a member of a parish? 1   2

35. Are you registered in that parish? 1   2

36. Approximately how much do you contribute to the church annually? (If married, include husband.)

    Circle the appropriate number

1	NOTHING	5	$751 - $1000
2	LESS THAN $250	6	$1000 - $2500
3	$251 - $500	7	$2500 - $5000
4	$501 - $750	8	OVER $5000

	ONCE A				
	DAY	WEEK	MONTH	IRREGULAR	NEVER

37. How often do you participate in the Eucharistic celebration (Mass), or Sunday Worship in your parish? 1   2   3   4   5

38. How often do you participate in the Eucharistic celebration (Mass), or Sunday Worship in another parish? 1   2   3   4   5

	YES	NO	SOMETIMES

39. Do you serve as a minister in your Parish? (i.e., Reader, Eucharist Minister, Music Minister, etc..) 1   2   3

    If so, NAME THE MINISTRIES _____

    If not, WHY _____

40. In what parish activities do you participate? (i.e., Fund Raising, Home and School Association, Altar/Rosary Society, etc.)

    _____

    _____

    _____

	YES	NO
41. Does your Parish have a Parish Council?	1	2
42. Does your Parish Council have any decision-making power?	1	2
43. Are you presently, or have you ever served, on the Parish Council?	1	2
44. If YES, do you feel you have an equal part with men in the decision-making process of the Parish Council?	1	2
45. Do you experience any significant difference between your decision-making power in your workplace and in your church life?	1	2

Explain: _____

_____

	YES	NO
46. Do you participate in a prayer group?	1	2
47. Is your prayer group a women's group?	1	2

48. Do you think of God as...

1	SPIRIT
2	HE/SHE
3	SHE
4	HE
5	OTHER

	YES	NO
49. Do you believe that Jesus wants men and women to be treated as equals?	1	2
50. Do you believe that you as a woman, are equal to a man?	1	2
51. Do you want to treated as equal to men?	1	2

	YES	NO	SOMETIMES
52. In your experience, do men treat you as an equal?	1	2	3

53. What specific hindrances do you meet in your efforts to be treated as equal to men?

		YES	NO
a.	FAMILY TRADITION	1	2
b.	LOW SELF-IMAGE	1	2
c.	MALE DOMINANCE	1	2
d.	SOCIAL MORES	1	2
e.	UNEQUAL COMPENSATION	1	2
f.	OTHER WOMEN	1	2
g.	ECONOMIC DEPENDENCE	1	2
h.	LACK OF EDUCATION	1	2

APPENDIX A

		YES	NO

54. Have you ever experienced personal rejection, ridicule, isolation or loneliness as you try to live the message of equality Jesus preached? 1 2

    Explain: _____

    _____

55. Do you believe that the equality of women and men is an integral part of the mission of Jesus? 1 2

56. Do you believe that Jesus wants women to be treated equal to men in the Church? 1 2

57. Do you believe that the message of Jesus regarding equality for women is practiced in the Catholic Church today? 1 2

58. Do your parish priests express Jesus' message regarding the equality of men and women in any of the following?

    a. PRAYERS OF THE FAITHFUL 1 2
    b. HOMILIES 1 2
    c. USE OF LANGUAGE INCLUDING WOMEN 1 2
    d. ATTITUDES/ACTIONS TOWARD WOMEN
       IN THE PARISH... 1 2

59. Are girls/women participating as altar servers, and/or homilists in your parish? 1 2

60. Would you like to see girls/women participating as altar servers, and/or homilists in your parish? 1 2

61. Would **You** like to participate as an:

    a. ALTAR SERVER 1 2
    b. HOMILIST 1 2
    c. DEACONESS 1 2

62. Are your hopes regarding the inclusion of women as ministers in your Sunday Liturgy fulfilled? 1 2

    If not, how do you find fulfillment? _____

    _____

63. Do you feel you deserve to be treated as an equal by the clergy? 1 2

64. In your recent experience, **have you been treated** as an equal by the clergy? 1 2

	YES	NO

65. Do you think your Pastor wants equal participation for women in the Church? 1 2

66. Describe how he conveys that message.

_____

_____

67. Do you think your Bishop wants equal participation for women in the Church? 1 2

68. Describe how he conveys that message.

_____

_____

69. Indicate any of the following you experience as obstacles in your efforts to minister in the Church?

		YES	NO
a.	CLERICALISM	1	2
b.	EXCLUSIVE LANGUAGE	1	2
c.	PATERNALISM	1	2
d.	MALE CHAUVINISM	1	2
e.	ATTITUDE OF BISHOP	1	2
f.	ATTITUDE OF ROME	1	2
g.	RACISM	1	2

70. Have you ever stopped attending Sunday Mass in a parish for any reason? (i.e., Poor liturgy, behavior of the priest, overemphasis on money, etc.) 1 2

Explain: _____

_____

71. Have you ever thought about withholding your financial support from your parish? 1 2

Explain: _____

72. Describe **your attitude** toward the clergy and hierarchy in general.

1 ANGRY   5 ACCEPTING
2 DISCOURAGED   6 FRIENDLY
3 INDIFFERENT   7 OTHER (specify) _____
4 DETACHED   _____

73. How would you describe the **attitude of the clergy** and or hierarchy toward you?

1 UNAPPRECIATIVE 5 ACCEPTING
2 HUMILIATING   6 FRIENDLY
3 PATRONIZING   7 OTHER (specify) _____
4 INDIFFERENT   _____

APPENDIX A

	YES	NO

74. What does "full participation" in the Church mean to you as a woman?

		YES	NO
a.	EQUAL DECISION-MAKING POWER WITH MEN?	1	2
b.	EQUAL ACCESS TO LEADERSHIP POSITIONS?	1	2
c.	EQUAL MINISTERIAL POSITIONS SUCH AS: READER, ALTAR SERVER, EUCHARISTIC MINISTER, ETC.	1	2
d.	EQUAL OPPORTUNITIES TO PREACH HOMILIES	1	2
e.	EQUAL ACCESS TO ORDINATION?	1	2

75. Do you identify with other women of the world who struggle for equality within the Church? 1   2

IF YES, what do you have in common with these women?

_____

_____

76. Would you like to learn more about these women? 1   2

	YES	NO	INDIFFERENT

77. Would you like to see women ordained as deaconesses or priests? 1   2   3

78. Would you like to be prepared for ordination? 1   2   3

79. Which of the following are you currently doing, or are willing to do, to obtain equality for women in the Church?

CURRENTLY DOING				WILLING TO DO	
YES	NO			YES	NO
1	2	.... a.	WRITE LETTERS	1	2
1	2	.... b.	SIGN PETITIONS	1	2
1	2	.... c.	PARTICIPATE IN WOMEN'S LITURGIES .	1	2
1	2	.... d.	CONTRIBUTE FINANCIAL SUPPORT	1	2
1	2	.... e.	JOIN WOMEN'S ORDINATION CONF......	1	2
1	2	.... f.	PARTICIPATE IN MARCHES	1	2
1	2	.... g.	PARTICIPATE IN BOYCOTTS	1	2
1	2	.... h.	WITHHOLD FINANCIAL SUPPORT	1	2
1	2	.... i.	NOTHING	1	2

80. Of those roles currently reserved to ordained men, which do you feel most called to do?

		YES	NO
a.	PRESIDE AT THE EUCHARIST	1	2
b.	ADMINISTER THE SACRAMENT OF RECONCILIATION	1	2
c.	ADMINISTER THE SACRAMENT OF THE SICK	1	2
d.	ADMINISTER THE SACRAMENT OF BAPTISM	1	2
e.	PRESIDE AT WEDDINGS	1	2
f.	PREACH AT THE LITURGY	1	2

	YES	NO	DON'T KNOW

81. Have you requested and been denied the opportunity to serve in a specific capacity within your parish or diocese? 1   2   3

Explain: (i.e. Chair the Parish Council, preach a Homily)

_____

_____

	YES	NO

82. If women could minister in the Church equally with men, would you think that Jesus' mission was being fulfilled? 1   2

Explain: _____

_____

_____

83. How do you feel about the degree of participation you as a woman have in the Catholic Church today?

Explain: _____

_____

_____

_____

_____

_____

_____

_____

Please sign below if you are interested in participating in an interview as a follow-up to this questionnaire.

NAME: _____

ADDRESS: _____

TELEPHONE: _____

APPENDIX B

Report on International Attitudes of Catholic Women
Prepared by
Rodney F. Ganey, Ph.D.
Social Science Training and Research Laboratory
University of Notre Dame

INTRODUCTION

The data for this analysis were collected by Sr. Francis B. O'Connor, C.S.C. The data comes from interviews and mail surveys from the countries presented below.

		Completed Surveys
Bangladesh	Parish Women	153
Brazil	Parish Women	408
Uganda	Parish Women	215
United States (Total)		485
	US Parish women	290
	US Women's Ordination Conference	83
	US Gallup Survey	112
Total Completed Surveys		1,261

The items included in this analysis were asked in the same way across all the countries where data are presented. Some questions were not asked in all of the countries and a few questions had a slightly different response framework across countries. Where these differences occur notations are provided. The US dataset was generated from 3 different subsamples. These were (1) a sample of representative parish women identified by women in the parishes, (2) women selected from the Women's Ordination Conference and, (3) Catholic women identified through a Gallup poll.

There are 5 key conceptual dimensions analyzed here. Each of the following sections describes a series of questions related to the topics listed below.

1. Equality with men
2. Jesus' message of equality in the Church
3. Obstacles to ministry
4. Ordination and support of other women
5. Meaning of full participation

The analysis will first look at the distribution of responses treating the data as one large dataset, then focus on differences between scores across each dataset, and finally collapsing the data into 4 groups; Bangladesh, Brazil, Uganda, and US women.

175

EQUALITY WITH MEN

There were 4 questions on this topic. The combined distribution is presented below.

(TABLE 1)

		Total % YES	Total % NO	Total % SOMETIMES
EQ1	Do you believe that Jesus wants men and women to be treated as equals?	97%	3%	
EQ2	Do you believe that you as a woman, are equal to a man?	79%	17%	4%
EQ3	Do you want to be treated as equal to men?	86%	11%	3%
EQ4	In your experience, do men treat you as an equal?	23%	47%	30%

Note questions 2 and 3 had a third category 'Sometimes' response for Uganda and question 4 had a 'Sometimes' response for all countries except Bangladesh and Brazil. The respondents strongly felt (97%) that Jesus wanted men and women to be equal although they felt not so strongly (79%) that they *were* equal or that they *want to be treated* as equal (86%). The most significant feature to the table is that only 23% of the women responding felt that they were, in fact, treated as equal, while 30% said this does occur sometimes. Forty-seven percent (47%) said they are *not* treated as equal. Therefore, there is a 33 percentage point difference (86% (23% + 30%)) of those who want to be treated as equal are not treated as equals and another 30% of those who want to be treated as equal are only treated as equal sometimes.

The distribution of scores from the individual datasets (table 2) shows remarkable consistency across countries on the first question (Jesus wants equality) but a great deal of diversity on the other questions. There is no significant difference in the scores across countries on EQ1 but there are statistically significant differences on all the remaining questions. Brazil, of the three non-US datasets, seems to reflect more of an attitude of equality than the other 2 non-US groups. The Brazilian women deeply feel that they should be more equal but when asked EQ4 they responded with a similar response to the women from Bangladesh which were much less supportive of the notion that they were equal to men (EQ2). The Ugandan women were the least positive toward notions of equality and were more likely to say that they were not treated as equals by men. The data is somewhat confused here because, of the 3 non-US countries, Uganda was the only country with a 'Sometimes' response category.

(TABLE 2)
DISTRIBUTION OF RESPONDENTS

		BANGLADESH	BRAZIL	UGANDA	HOLY CROSS MEMBERS	HOLY CROSS AFFILIATES/FORMER	US PARISH	US WOMEN'S ORDINATION CONF	US GALLUP
EQ1	Yes	98%	98%	94%	97%	97%	97%	100%	92%
	No	2%	2%	6%	3%	3%	3%	—	8%
	N=	(146)	(401)	(211)	(433)	(249)	(275)	(83)	(108)
EQ2	Yes	70%	83%	61%	95%	95%	86%	100%	82%
	No	30%	17%	18%	5%	5%	14%	—	18%
	Sometimes	—	—	21%	—	—	—	—	—
	N=	(135)	(393)	(212)	(413)	(254)	(275)	(82)	(108)
EQ3	Yes	80%	92%	70%	95%	95%	91%	100%	81%
	No	20%	8%	14%	5%	5%	9%	—	19%
	Sometimes	—	—	16%	—	—	—	—	—
	N=	(142)	(386)	(213)	(395)	(247)	(263)	(80)	(103)
EQ4	Yes	31%	29%	5%	41%	30%	24%	14%	29%
	No	69%	71%	62%	7%	12%	16%	11%	13%
	Sometimes	—	—	33%	52%	58%	60%	75%	58%
	N=	(137)	(361)	(211)	(408)	(250)	(280)	(79)	(108)

The Gallup derived sample of the US Catholic women was the *least* supportive group to question EQ1 of all the 8 datasets. This group represents the least selected members, but even here, 92% of all respondents said that Jesus wanted equality and 82%, a similar percentage as Brazil, said that they felt they were equal to men. This is the lowest percentage of all the US groups. Further, the Gallup sample had the lowest percentage of women responding that they wanted to be treated as equal to men (81%). This is consistent with the data from Bangladesh and only higher than Uganda in these data. The other US data was at the 91% or higher level. The Women's Ordination Conference was somewhat more likely not to perceive their treatment by men as equal all the time (14% versus an average of about 30% for the other groups), but they were roughly consistent with the other US data in having 11% responding negatively to the question. The largest group of US respondents responded with 'Sometimes' to the question. The Bangladesh and Brazil data did not include a 'Sometimes' response category and the scores from these 2 countries ran about identical with about 30% responding yes and 70% responding no, that they were not treated as equal. In essence the percent 'Yes' is about the same as the US data but the percent 'No' is the combined total of 'Sometimes' and 'No' in the US data. In Uganda where 'Sometimes' was used the percentage responding 'Yes' was the lowest of all the sets (5%). Sixty-one percent (62%) said 'No' and 33% said 'Sometimes'. The 'Sometimes' group seems to have pulled cases away from the 'Yes' response category and did not affect the 'No' response category. Making the 'No response consistent with the other non-US dataset but suppressing the 'Yes' response group to the lowest of all the datasets.

Jesus' Message of Equality In the Church

There were 6 questions on this topic. The combined distribution is presented below.

(TABLE 3)

		Total % YES	Total % NO	Total % SOMETIMES
EQC1	Do you believe that the equality of women and men is an integral part of the mission of Jesus?	91%	9%	
EQC2	Do you believe that Jesus wants women to be treated equal to men in the Church?	94%	6%	
EQC3	Do you believe that the message of Jesus regarding equality for women is practiced in the Catholic Church today?	42%	54%	4%

	Total % YES	Total % NO	Total % DON'T KNOW
EQC4 Do you think your priest wants equal participation for women in the Church?	68%	4%	8%
EQC5 Do you think your bishop wants equal participation for women in the Church?	46%	36%	18%

Respondents generally believe that the equality of men and women (EQC1) is an integral part of the mission of Jesus. This question was asked only to US sample members and 91% agreed. The lowest level of agreement was again in the Gallup respondents where only 77% agreed. Across all countries respondents believed that Jesus wants women to be treated as equal to men (EQC2). Ninety-four percent agreed to this statement. The message of equality (EQC3) is not generally practiced in the Church today according to these data. Note the levels of agreement below.

(TABLE 4)

	% Agreement to EQC3
Bangladesh	51%
Brazil	61%
Uganda	45%
US Parish women	22%
US Women's Ordination Conference	4%
US Gallup survey	32%

Clearly this does not show consistency with the message indicated in the first two questions of this section.

The priests are perceived as wanting more equality (EQC4). Although across the 8 datasets there is quite a bit of variation with 86% agreeing in Brazil but only 38% agreeing in Uganda. The US. response is fairly consistent with a range from 61% in the Women's Ordination Conference sample and 73% in the US Gallup sample. Note that the Uganda dataset did reflect a 36% response of 'Don't Know'. This is probably adding to the low agreement level in this data. Further, while the level of agreement was above 60% in all the US samples, the level of disagreement was also high. Disagreement on EQC4 ranged from 39% in the Women's Ordination Conference to 27% in the Gallup dataset. The bishops are perceived across all of these data to be less supportive than the priests of equality (EQC5). Overall only 40% agreed that the bishops were supportive. Brazil had the highest level of bishops' support (64%) and in the US Gallup group 54% said bishops were supportive. Where an option was given for 'Don't know' (Bangladesh and Uganda) significant numbers of respondents, 40% and 51% respectively, selected this option for EQC5.

OBSTACLES TO MINISTRY

There were 4 questions on this topic (EQC6 having 7 parts). The combined distribution is presented below.

(TABLE 5)

		Total % YES	Total % NO
EQC6A	Clericalism	62%	38%
EQC6B	Exclusive language	56%	44%
EQC6C	Paternalism	67%	33%
EQC6D	Male chauvinism	71%	29%
EQC6E	Attitude of bishop	62%	38%
EQC6F	Attitude of Rome	77%	23%
EQC6G	Racism	38%	62%

		Total % YES	Total % NO	Total % DON'T KNOW
EQC7	Have you ever stopped attending Sunday Mass in a parish for any reason? (ie. Poor liturgy, behavior of the priest, overemphasis on money, etc.)	49%	51%	
EQC8	Have you ever thought about withholding your financial support from your parish?	34%	66%	
EQC9	Have you requested and been denied the opportunity to serve in a specific capacity within your parish or diocese?	12%	83%	5%

These questions were only asked of the US samples. Respondents were asked to identify which of the following (EQ6A EQC6G) they experience as obstacles in efforts to minister in the Church. Note that the most significant problem indicated is the attitude of Rome (77%) followed closely by male chauvinism (71%), and paternalism (67%). Attitudes of the bishop (67%), clericalism (62%) and exclusive language (56%) also rated high in importance. The least significant problem in this list was racism (38%).

Below is the 3 dataset breakdown of agreement to the following obstacles.

(TABLE 6)

	1 USP	2 USWOC	3 USG
Clericalism	56%	94%	39%
Exclusive language	46%	93%	33%
Paternalism	61%	97%	42%
Male chauvinism	69%	94%	48%
Attitude of Rome	72%	96%	67%
Racism	33%	64%	19%

Clearly the Gallup group had the lowest percentage of these problems, but they are the group least likely to be active in church activities. The second least active group are the parish women in group 1. Note that in this group better than 50% respond that there are significant obstacles in all cases except racism.

An additional set of 3 questions was asked of all US samples which addresses the issue of obstacles to participation. These questions are particularly revealing because they relate to the elasticity of demand for services based on obstacles to participation . The first question relates to stopping attending Mass. Note that 49% indicate they have, in fact, stopped attending Mass at some point due to perceived problems. Thirty-four percent (34%) indicate they have withheld financial support, but there is a very wide range of agreement across the 3 datasets. Only 12% indicate they have been denied the opportunity to serve in the parish. The following table breaks out the level of agreement in each of the 3 datasets.

(TABLE 7)

	1 USP	2 USWOC	3 USG
EQC7	41%	77%	50%
EQC8	29%	69%	24%
EQC9	9%	27%	8%

Note that by far the women in the Women's Ordination Conference group indicates the highest level of obstacles to participation. They have withdrawn support in the past and have also been denied access in the past.

ORDINATION AND SUPPORT OF OTHER WOMEN

There were 5 questions on this topic. The combined distribution is presented below.

(TABLE 8)

		Total % YES	Total % NO	Total % INDIFFERENT
SO1	Do you identify with other women of the world who struggle for equality within the Church?	70%	30%	
SO2	Would you like to learn more about these women?	90%	10%	
SO3	Would you like to see women ordained as deaconesses or priests?	61%22%	17%	
SO4	Would you like to be prepared for ordination?	25%	65%	10%
SO5	Would you support other women who want to be trained for ordination? (ie. through prayer or encouragement)	83%	17%	

Agreement with the identification issue (SO1) was strongest among the non-US samples and the US Women's Ordination Conference sample.

Women in the Church tend to support other women in their efforts to achieve equality in the Church. This is true of a majority of women in all groups except the Gallup sample where only 34% agreed to this statement. Overall 66% agreed, with 86% of the Women's Ordination Conference sample agreeing and respectively Bangladesh, Brazil and Uganda reporting agreement of 82%, 72% and 76%. There is also strong support for finding out more about women's efforts from other countries in all of the groups except the Gallup sample, where only 40% agreed to question SO2.

There was general support for women to be ordained as deaconesses or priests in all of the samples except Bangladesh. The Bangladesh sample reported only 41% agreement to question SO3 while 59% disagreed. Across all the datasets the highest support for women training for ordination was found in the non-US data, with the exception of the Women's Ordination Conference data, where 39% support it. Overall only 25% supported their own preparation for ordination. Although if women did want to be trained they would find a supportive group, as indicated in SO5 where 83% indicated they would support these women. Note, SO5 was only asked of the samples from Bangladesh, Brazil and Uganda.

MEANING OF FULL PARTICIPATION

There were 7 questions on this topic. The combined distribution is presented below.

(TABLE 9)

		Total % YES	Total % NO
	YES	NO	
What does "full participation" in the Church mean to you as a woman?			
SO6	Equal decision-making power with men	83%	17%
SO7	Equal access to leadership positions	77%	23%
SO8	Equal ministerial positions such as: reader, altar server, eucharistic minister, etc.	81%	19%
SO9	Equal opportunities to preach homilies	67%	33%
SO10	Equal access to the diaconate	38%	62%
SO11	Equal access to priesthood	52%	48%
SO12	How do you feel about the degree of participation you as a woman have in the Catholic Church today? Would you like to have more opportunities to participate?	81%	19%

Full participation means different things to different women. The clearest support is for equality in decision making power, access to ministerial positions and access to leadership positions. There is also strong support for opportunities to preach homilies (67%). The overall analysis shows an almost equally divided response to the equal access to the priesthood question (SO11). Fifty-two percent (52%) support equal access while 48% do not support it. The table below displays the range of agreement to this question across the 6 datasets.

(TABLE 10)

	Agreement that full participation means equal access to the priesthood
Bangladesh	28%
Brazil	46%
Uganda	33%
US Parish women	65%
US Women's Ordination Conference	98%
US Gallup survey	53%

It is interesting to note that while all the US based samples had better than 50% positive response to this question, none of the three non US samples had over 50% positive response to this question.

The last question in this section indicates that women in general want more participation in the Church. The question was asked of only the three non US groups; Bangladesh, Brazil, and Uganda. Note the distribution below.

(TABLE 11)

	Agreement that respondents want more participation in the Church
Bangladesh	78%
Brazil	77%
Uganda	90%

Note the high level of agreement in the non US groups, especially in the Uganda sample.

APPENDIX C

Comparison of Women's Responses to Four Key Questions

Full Participation for women means...

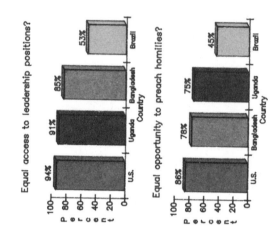

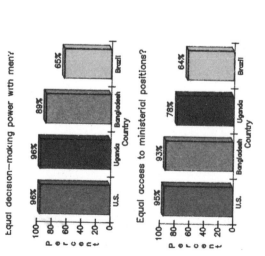

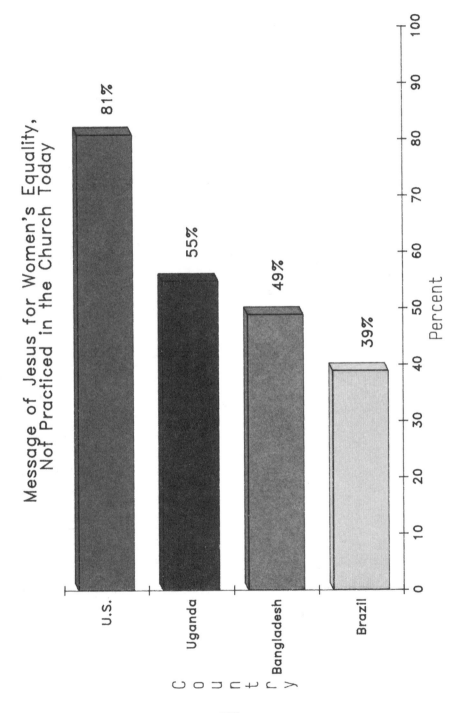

Message of Jesus for Women's Equality,
Not Practiced in the Church Today

81%

55%

49%

39%

Percent

U.S.

Uganda

Bangladesh

Brazil

Country

LIKE BREAD, THEIR VOICES RISE!

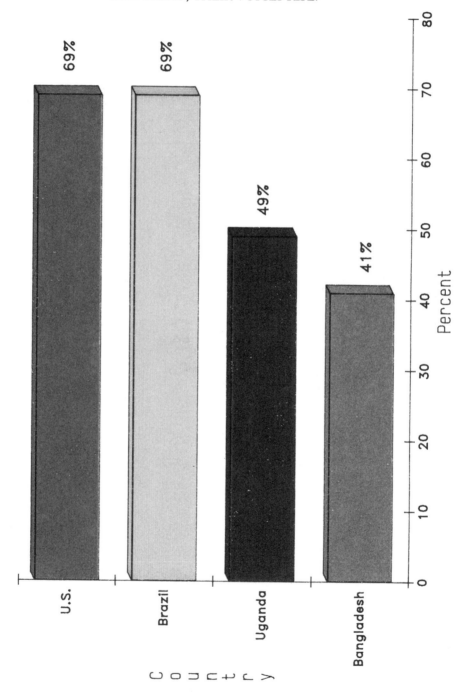

In Favor of Ordination for Women

U.S. 69%
Brazil 69%
Uganda 49%
Bangladesh 41%

Country

Percent

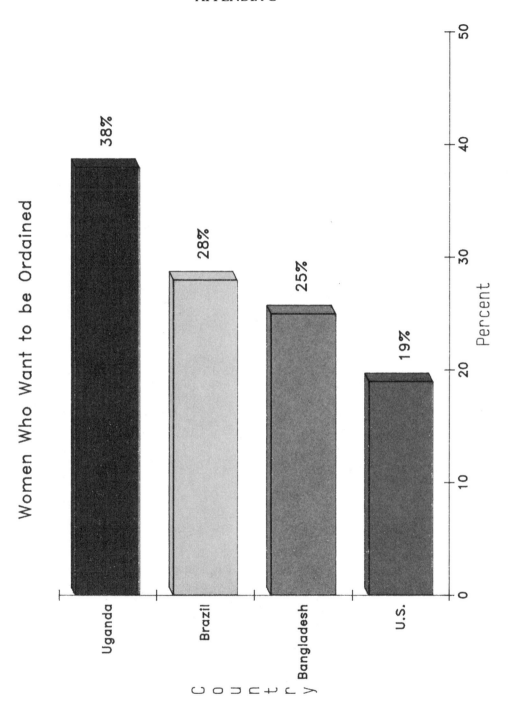

Women Who Want to be Ordained

NOTES

DEDICATION

[1] Adapted from Miriam Therese Winter, "A Psalm in Praise of Anonymous Women," *WomanWord*, New York: The Crossroad Publishing Company, 1990, pp. 116-117.

INTRODUCTION

[1] Sister Martha Ann Kirk, "Prison," *Images of Women in Transition*, Compiled by Janice Grana, Winona, MN: St. Mary's Press, 1991, p. 114.

[2] Mary C. Boys, "Life on the Margins: Feminism and Religious Education," *Initiatives*, Washington, DC: National Association for Women in Education, 1992, p. 19.

Chapter 1 WOMEN, WHY DO WE WEEP?

[1] Winter, "A Psalm for Women Who Weep," *WomanWord*, p. 147.

[2] Adapted from Leonard Swidler, *Biblical Affirmations of Woman*, Philadelphia, PA: Westminster Press, 1979, p. 192.

[3] Joann Wolski Conn, "A Discipleship of Equals: Past, Present, and Future," *Horizons*, Volume 14-2, 1987, pp. 231-261.

[4] David C. Leege and Thomas A. Trozzolo, "Participation in Catholic Parish Life: Religious Rites and Parish Activities in the 1980s," *Notre Dame Study of Catholic Parish Life*, Report No. 3, Notre Dame, IN: University of Notre Dame, December, 1984, p. 3. Updated figures taken from *The Official Catholic Directory*, New Providence, RI: P.J. Kenedy & Sons, 1992, p. 36.

[5] David C. Leege and Thomas A. Trozzolo, Report No. 3, pp. 7-8.

[6] David C. Leege, "Parish Life Among the Leaders," *Notre Dame Study of Catholic Parish Life*, Report No. 9, Notre Dame, IN: University of Notre Dame, December, 1989, p. 15.

[7] Jay P. Dolan and David C. Leege, "A Profile of American Catholic Parishes and Parishioners: 1820s to the 1980s," *Notre Dame Study of Catholic Parish Life*, Report No. 2, Notre Dame, IN: University of Notre Dame, February, 1985, p. 8.

[8] Maria Riley, *In God's Image*, Kansas City, MO: Sheed and Ward, 1985, p. 24.

[9] Adapted from Joan Chittister's commencement address at Saint Mary's College, Notre Dame, IN, May, 1991.

[10] See "On the Dignity and Vocation of Women" (*Mulieris Dignitatem*), Apostolic Letter, August 15, 1988.

[11] Marcello Azevedo, *Vocation for Mission*, New York: Paulist Press, 1988, p. 155.

[12] Gerda Lerner, *The Creation of Patriarchy*, New York: Oxford University Press, 1986, p. 218.

[13] Mary Jo Weaver, *New Catholic Women: A Contemporary Challenge to Traditional Religious Authority*, San Francisco: Harper and Row, 1985, p. 169.

[14] Pax Christi, *Peacemaking Day by Day*, Volume II, Erie, PA: Benet Press, 1989, p. 54.

[15] Dolores L. Greeley, "Patriarchy: A Global Reality," *Where Can We Find Her? Searching for Women's Identity in the New Church*, Marie-Eloise Rosenblatt, ed., New York: Paulist Press, 1991, p. 89.

[16] As taken from Rosemary R. Ruether, "Feminism and Religious Faith: Renewal or Creation?" *Religion and Intellectual Life 3*, Winter, 1986, as cited in Sandra Schneiders' *Beyond Patching*, p. 34.

[17] Ibid., p. 34. Sandra Schneiders credits Elisabeth Schussler Fiorenza and Maria Riley with this Christian/Catholic feminist view for those who choose to remain within the faith tradition, and who believe the transformation of the church beyond patriarchy is the enduring agenda.

[18] Winter, "Prayer," *WomanWord* p. 146.

Chapter 2 WHO CARES ABOUT US?

[1] Miriam Therese Winter, "A Psalm for Shedding Pretenses," *WomanWisdom*, New York: The Crossroad Publishing Company, 1991, p. 202.

[2] Miria R.K. Matembe, "The Situation of Women in Uganda," Keynote Address given at N.C.R. Women Representatives' Seminar, Jinja, Uganda, June 12-13, 1990, p. 9.

[3] *Children and Women in Uganda: A Situation Analysis*, United Nations Children's Fund, Kampala, Uganda, 1989. Demographic and geographical information taken from this source.

[4] Taken in part from the *Chicago Tribune*, "Economic Victims," by Jane Perlez, April 21, 1991, Section 6, p. 8.

[5] Matembe, p. 5.

[6] *Children and Women in Uganda: A Situation Analysis*, UNICEF, Preface.

[7] Joan Kakwenzire, "Women and Human Rights in Uganda," *Arise*, a women's developmental magazine, Kampala, Uganda: Acfode Publishing Company, April-June, 1991, p. 13.

[8] Abby J. Nalwanga-Sebina and Dr. Edith R. Natukunda, "Uganda Women's Needs Assessment Survey 1988," a research study of 685 rural women, Kampala, Uganda: Makerere University, p. 119.

[9] Rodrigo Mejia, "Presence of the Lay Christians in the Preparation for the Synod of Bishops in Africa," *AFER (African Ecclesial Review), Appeal to the African Synod,* Vol. 33, No. 4, August, 1991, Eldoret, Kenya: AMECEA Gaba Pastoral Institute, p. 173.

[10] Sister Anna Mary Mukamuwezi, "Church Moral Teaching and the Dignity of an African Woman," Social Justice Newsletter, Issue No. 3, August, 1991, p. 11.

[11] Mejia, p. 172.

[12] Virginia Fabella and Mercy Amba Oduyoye, ed., *With Passion and Compassion*, Maryknoll, New York: Orbis Books, 1989, p. 11.

[13] Michael H. Crosby, *The Dysfunctional Church*, Notre Dame, IN: Ave Maria Press, 1991, p. 115.

[14] Bernadette Kunambi, "The Place of Women in the Christian Community," *African Christian Spirituality*, ed. by Aylward Shorter, London, England: A Geoffrey Chapman book, published by Cassel Ltd., 1978, p. 154.

[15] Fabella and Oduyoye, p. 42.

[16] Rosemary Haughton, *The Re-Creation of Eve*, Springfield, IL: Templegate Publishers, 1985, p. 1.

[17] Ibid., p. 4.

[18] Fabella and Oduyoye, p. xiv.

[19] Winter, "Because- I -Am- a-Woman Psalm," *Woman Wisdom*, p. 293.

Chapter 3 DON'T SILENCE US!

[1] Winter, "A Psalm of Wise Words," *WomanWisdom*, p. 354.

[2] *Courier*, Dhaka, Bangladesh, February 14-20, 1992, p. 19.

[3] Salma Khan, *The Fifty Percent: Women in Development and Policy in Bangladesh*, Dhaka, Bangladesh: University Press, Ltd., 1988, p. 1.

[4] Santi Rozario, "Marginality and the cause of unmarried Christian women in a Bangladeshi village," *Contributions to Indian Sociology*, New Delhi: Sage Publications, 1986, p. 267.

[5] Ibid., p. 271.

[6] Salma Khan, p. 132.

[7] Ibid., pp. 108-110.

[8] As quoted in Malladi Subbamma, *Women, Tradition and Culture*, Dhaka, Bangladesh: United Press Ltd., 1985, p. 9.

[9] Patricia Jeffery, *Frogs in a Well: Indian Women in Purdah*, New Delhi: Vikas Publishing House Pvt. Ltd., 1979, p. 11, and Malladi Subbamma, *Women, Tradition and Culture*, p. 32, for a description of Indian women characterized as "frogs in a well."

[10] Virginia Fabella, "Mission of Women in the Church in Asia: Role and Position," AMOR VII, Seoul, Korea, October, 1985, pp. 1-7.

[11] Malladi Subbamma, pp. 10-11.

[12] Benedicta Leonilla Ageira, "Communion: Role of Women," *Vidyajyoti Journal of Theological Reflection*, Vol. 54, No. 5, May, 1990, p. 245.

[13] Flavia D'Souza, "Women Live Their Faith in a Sexist Church," *Jeevadhara, A Journal of Christian Interpretation*, May, 1990, p. 187.

[14] Richard P. McBrien, "The Church of Tomorrow," *Women in Religion*, edited by Regina Coll, New York: Paulist Press, 1982, p. 135.

[15] Rabindranath Tagore, *Gitanjali*, translated by Brother James Talarovic, Dhaka, Bangladesh: University Press Limited, 1983, p. 115, edited.

Chapter 4   RISE UP WOMEN!

[1] Winter, "A Liberation Psalm for Women," *WomanWord*, p. 138.

[2] "Brazil: Women Respond to Bishops' Campaign," Latinamerica Press, April 12, 1990, p. 5.

[3] Quoted in Marianne Katoppo, *Compassionate and Free*, Maryknoll, NY: Orbis Books, 1980, pp. 63-64.

[4] Leonardo Boff, *Ecclesiogenesis: The Base Communities Reinvent the Church*, Maryknoll, NY: Orbis Books, 1986, p. 78.

[5] *Brazil*, American Friends Service Committee, Philadelphia, PA, 1985.

[6] "Educacao: A maquena que cospecriancas" ("Education: The machine that spits out children"), *VEJA*, 20 de Novembro, 1991.

[7] Shulamit Goldsmit and Ernest Sweeney, "The Church and Latin American Women in Their Struggle for Equality and Justice," *Thought*, Vol. 63, No. 249 (June 1988), pp. 176-77. "The concept of a masculine world, ruled by men and in which women merely play a passive role, stems from Mesopotamian and Judeo-Mediterranean patriarchal societies in which all socio-political power resided in the male. Those societies also fostered an exclusively male image of God. This tradition of patriarchal dominance in Western civiliza-

tion was transmitted to Latin America through the Iberian-Arabic culture of its conquerors, and was reinforced by the Catholic Church."

[8] Elsa Tamez, *Against Machismo*, Oak Park, IL: Meyer Stone, 1987, p. vii.

[9] Ibid., pp. 109-10.

[10] Boff, p. 61.

[11] Ibid, pp. 3-4.

[12] Quoted in Alvaro Barreiro, *Basic Ecclesial Communities: The Evangelization of the Poor*, translated from Portuguese by Barbara Campbell, Maryknoll, NY: Orbis Books, 1982, p. 37.

[13] Tamez, p. 137.

[14] Elsa Tamez, ed., *Through Her Eyes: Women's Theology from Latin America*, "Reflections on the Trinity," by Maria Clara Bingemer, Maryknoll, NY: Orbis Books, 1989. pp. 71-72.

[15] Barreiro, p. 8.

[16] Goldsmit and Sweeney, p. 182.

[17] Sonia E. Alvarez, *Feminist Studies*, Vol. 16, No. 2, Summer 1990.

[18] Goldsmit and Sweeney, pp. 182-83.

[19] Boff, p. 89.

[20] Elizabeth Gossman, "Women as Priests?" in *Apostolic Succession: Rethinking a Barrier to Unity*, ed. Hans Kung, *Concilium*, Vol. 34, New York: Paulist Press, 1968, pp. 122-23.

[21] Quoted in Alvarez, p. 381.

[22] Boff, pp. 93-95.

[23] Ibid, p. 81.

[24] Winter, p. 138.

Chapter 5 HOW LONG MUST WE WAIT?

[1] Miriam Therese Winter, "A Psalm for Those Passed Over," *WomanWitness*, New York: The Crossroad Publishing Company, 1992, p. 251.

[2] Barbel von Wartenberg-Potter, *We Will Not Hang Our Harps on the Willows*, translated by Fred Kaan, Geneva, Switzerland: World Council of Churches, 1987, p. 40.

[3] Marcello Azevedo, *Vocation for Mission: The Challenge of Religious Life Today*, New York: Paulist Press, 1986, pp. 153-54.

[4] Richard P. McBrien, Keynote Address, National Convention of CORPUS, Chicago, IL, June 12, 1992.

[5] Crosby, p. 81.

[6] Mary Jo Leddy, "Beyond Nagging: The Prophetic Role of Women in the Church," *Catholic New Times*, November 6, 1988.

[7] Evelyn and Frank Stagg, *Women in the World of Jesus*, Philadelphia, PA: Westminster Press, 1978, p. 115.

[8] Kenneth L. Woodward with Mary Lord, "A Sister Speaks Up," *Newsweek*, October 22, 1979, p. 125.

[9] Constance F. Parvey, ed., *The Community of Women and Men in the Church, The Sheffield Report*, Geneva: World Council of Churches, 1983, p. 77.

[10] von Wartenberg-Potter, p. 52.

Chapter 6 BREAKING THE SILENCE

[1] Winter, "A Psalm for Keeping Faith," *WomanWisdom*, p. 169.

[2] "Bishops Told Women Impatient with Church Apathy Toward Women's Problems,"*The Herald*, Calcutta, India, February 7-13, 1992.

[3] Chitra Fernando, "The Role of the Church in the Oppression of Women," in *The Emerging Christian Woman*, S. Faria, A.V. Alexander, and J.B. Tellis-Nayak, editors. Pune, India: Salprakashan Sanchar Kendra/Ishwani, 1984, pp. 61-62.

[4] "A Report," presented by Mukti Barton, Director of Netritto Proshikkhon Kendro (Women's Ecumenical Leadership Training Center), Dhaka, Bangladesh, 1988-91.

[5] Rabindranath Tagore, *Collected Poems and Plays*. London: Macmillan, 1971, p. 16 (last line changed from, "let my country awake").

Chapter 7 OUT OF THE KITCHEN

[1] Winter, "A Psalm of Confidence," *WomanWisdom.*, p. 328.

[2] Daniel Wabwire, "Liberation for the African Woman," *New People*, No. 17, March-April, 1992, p. 3.

[3] "Contribution of the Religious Congregations of Women in Uganda to the African Synod," Kampala, Uganda: Association Religeosarum Ugandae (ARU), 1991, p. 1.

[4] R. Modupe Owanikin, "The Priesthood of Church Women in the Nigerian Context," in *The Will to Arise*, Mercy Amba Oduyoye and Musimbi R. A. Kanyoro, ed., Maryknoll, NY: Orbis, 1992, pp. 226-27.

[5] Susan Muto, *Womanspirit*, New York: The Crossroad Publishing Company, 1991, p. 11.

[6] Sister Anne Nasimiyu Wasi, "Women in the Catholic Church," *New People*, Nairobi, Kenya: Media Centre, September-October, 1991, p. 20.

[7] Teresa Okure, "The Will to Arise: Reflections on Luke 8:40-56," *The Will to Arise*, p. 230.

[8] Reprinted, with changes, from Winter, "A Psalm Celebrating a Royal Priesthood," *WomanWitness*, p. 76.

Chapter 8 SET US FREE!

[1] Reprinted, with changes, from Winter, "A Psalm of Freedom," *WomanWisdom*, p. 122.

[2] Barbel von Wartenberg-Potter, *We Will Not Hang our Harps on the Willows*, translated by Fred Kaan, Geneva, Switzerland: World Council of Churches, 1987, p. 73.

[3] Ibid., p. 54.

[4] Winter, pp. 122-23.

Chapter 9 WEAVING WOMEN'S VISIONS

[1] Marsie Silvestro, "I am a Woman Weaver," *Crossing the Lines*, Recorded at the Loft, Lips Music Inc., Bronxville, New York, adapted.

[2] Barbel von Wartenberg-Potter, p. 77.

[3] Marilyn Sewell, ed., "Owning Self," *Cries of the Spirit*, Boston: Beacon Press, 1991, p. 19.

[4] Rosemary Radford Ruether, "Motherearth and the Megamachine: A Theology of Liberation in a Feminine, Somatic and Ecological Perspective," in *Womanspirit Rising*, Carol P. Christ and Judith Plaskow, ed., San Francisco: Harper and Row, Publishers, 1979, p. 44.

[5] Marcia Froelke Coburn, as taken from, "First Lady role isn't One-size-fits-all," *Chicago Tribune*, August 16, 1992.

[6] Dolores L. Greeley, "Patriarchy: A Global Reality," in *Where Can We Find Her?* Marie-Eloise Rosenblatt, ed., New York: Paulist Press, 1991, p. 86.

[7] Sheila Collins, "Theology in the Politics of Appalachian Women," in *Womanspirit Rising*, p. 157.

[8] Regina Coll, "The Socialization of Women into a Patriarchal System," *Women in Religion*, Regina Coll, ed., New York: Paulist Press, 1982, p. 12.

[9] Lois W. Banner, *Elizabeth Cady Stanton: A Radical for Women's Rights*, Oscar Handlin, ed., Boston: Little Brown and Company, 1980, p. 157.

[10] von Wartenberg-Potter, p. 99.

[11] Rosemary Haughton, p. 12.

[12] von Wartenberg-Potter, p. 46.

[13] Elisabeth Schussler Fiorenza, "Feminist Spirituality, Christian Identity, and Catholic Vision," in *Womanspirit Rising*, p. 147.

[14] Rosemary Haughton, p. 144.

[15] Bill Huebsch, *A New Look at Prayer*, Mystic, CT: Twenty-Third Publications, 1991, p. 99.

[16] "Bishops Told Women Impatient with Church Apathy Toward Women's Problems," *The Herald*.

[17] Virginia Fabella and Mercy Amba Oduyoye, eds., "Final Document: Intercontinental Women's Conference," *With Passion and Compassion*, p. 187.

[18] Virginia Fabella, "A Common Methodology for Diverse Christologies?" *With Passion and Compassion*, p. 117.

[19] Marsie Silvestro, "I am a Woman Weaver."

Chapter 10 LET THERE BE BREAD!

[1] Carter Heyward, "Litany of the Bread," *Our Passion for Justice: Images of Power, Sexuality, and Liberation*, Cleveland, OH: The Pilgrim Press, 1984.

[2] Rachel Conrad Wahlberg, *Jesus According to a Woman*, New York: Paulist Press, 1975, p. 97.

[3] Rosemary Haughton, p. 81.

[4] Mary Jo Weaver, p. 64.

[5] Peter Hebblethwaite, "Despite Vatican, Women on World Agenda," *National Catholic Reporter*, Kansas City, MO: June 7, 1991, p. 6.

[6] "Called to be One in Christ Jesus," Third Draft/Pastoral on Concerns of Women, *Origins*, Vol. 21, No. 46, April 23, 1992, p. 768.

[7] Alicia Craig Faxon, *Women and Jesus*, Philadelphia: United Church Press, 1973, p. 116.

[8] Gerda Lerner, p. 217.

[9] Bishop P. Francis Murphy, "Let's Start Over," *Commonweal*, September 25, 1992, p. 13.

[10] Caroline Julia Bartlett, "Woman's Call to the Ministry," *Cries of the Spirit*, p. 248.

[11] Richard P. McBrien, "The Feminization of Parish Ministry" (syndicated column), *The Church World*, Portland, ME, August 27, 1992.

[12] Walbert Buhlmann, *With Eyes to See: Church and World in the Third Millennium*, Maryknoll, NY: Orbis Books, 1990, p. 6.

[13] Rosemary Haughton, *Song in a Strange Land*, Springfield, IL: Templegate Publishers, 1990, p. 50.

[14] Dorothy Vidulich, "Sisters say new nuns group could spell trouble," *National Catholic Reporter*, Kansas City, MO, Vol. 28, No. 33, July 3, 1992, p. 7.

[15] Bishop P. Francis Murphy, p. 14.

[16] Walter M. Abbott, ed., "Gaudium et Spes," *The Documents of Vatican II*, New York: America Press, 1966, pp. 201-202.

[17] Richard P. McBrien, "Strategies for Survival" (syndicated column), *The Church World*, Portland, ME, August 20, 1992.

BIBLIOGRAPHY

Abbott, Walter M, ed. "Pastoral Constitution on the Church in the Modern World." *The Documents of Vatican II.* New York: America Press, 1966.

Ageira, Benedicta Leonilla. "Communion: Role of Women." *Vidyajyoti Journal of Theological Reflection.* Vol. 54, No. 5, May, 1990.

Alvarez, Sonia E. *Feminist Studies.* Vol. 16, No. 2, Summer 1990.

Azevedo, Marcello. *Vocation for Mission: The Challenge of Religious Life Today.* New York: Paulist Press, 1988.

Banner, Lois W. *Elizabeth Cady Stanton: A Radical for Women's Rights.* Oscar Handlin, ed., Boston: Little Brown & Company, 1980.

Barlett, Caroline Julia. "Woman's Call to the Ministry." *Cries of the Spirit.* Marilyn Sewell ed., Boston: Beacon Press, 1991.

Barton, Mukti. "A Report." Dhaka, Bangladesh, 1988-91.

Barreiro, Alvaro. *Basic Ecclesial Communities: The Evangelization of the Poor.* Translated from Portuguese by Barbara Campbell. Maryknoll, NY: Orbis Books, 1982.

"Bishops Told Women Impatient with Church Apathy Toward Women's Problems." *The Herald.* Calcutta Diocesan Newspaper: February 7-13, 1992.

Boff, Leonardo. *Ecclesiogenesis: The Base Communities Reinvent the Church.* Maryknoll, NY: Orbis Books, 1986.

Boys, Mary C. "Life on the Margins: Feminism and Religious Education." *Initiatives.* Washington, DC: National Association for Women in Education, 1992.

Brazil. American Friends Service Committee. Philadelphia, PA, 1985.

"Brazil: Women Respond to Bishops' Campaign." Latinamerica Press, April 12, 1990.

Buhlmann, Walbert. *With Eyes to See: Church and World in the Third Millennium.* Maryknoll, NY: Orbis Books, 1990.

"Called to be One in Christ Jesus." Third Draft/Pastoral on Concerns of Women. *Origins.* Vol. 21, No. 46, April 23, 1992.

Children and Women in Uganda: A Situation Analysis. United Nations Children's Fund. Kampala, Uganda, 1989.

Chittister, Joan. Commencement Address. Notre Dame, IN: Saint Mary's College. May, 1991.

Christ, Carol P. and Judith Plaskow, eds. *Womanspirit Rising*. San Francisco: Harper and Row Publishers, 1979.

Coburn, Marcia Froelke. As taken from "First Lady role isn't One-size-fits-all." *Chicago Tribune*. August 16, 1992.

Coll, Regina. "The Socialization of Women into a Patriarchal System." *Women in Religion*. Regina Coll, ed. New York: Paulist Press, 1982.

Collins, Sheila. "Theology in the Politics of Appalachian Women." *Womanspirit Rising*. Carol P. Christ and Judith Plaskow eds. San Francisco: Harper and Row Publishers, 1979.

Conn, Joann Wolski. "A Discipleship of Equals: Past, Present and Future." *Horizons*. Vol. 14, No. 2, 1987.

"Contribution of the Religious Congregations of Women in Uganda to the African Synod." Kampala, Uganda: Association Religeosarum Ugandae (ARU), 1991.

Courier. Dhaka, Bangladesh, February 14-20, 1992.

Crosby, Michael H. *The Dysfunctional Church*. Notre Dame, IN: Ave Maria Press, 1991.

Dolan, Jay P. and David Leege. "A Profile of American Catholic Parishes and Parishioners: 1820s to the 1980s." *Notre Dame Study of Catholic Parish Life*. Report No. 2. Notre Dame, IN: University of Notre Dame, February, 1985.

D'Souza, Flavia. "Women Live Their Faith in a Sexist Church." *Jeevadhara ,A Journal of Christian Interpretation*. May, 1990.

"Educacao: A maquena que cospecriancas" ("Education: The machine that spits out children"). *VEJA*. 20 de Novembro, 1991.

Fabella, Virginia. "Mission of Women in the Church in Asia: Role and Position." *AMOR*. VII. Seoul, Korea, October 1985.

Fabella, Virginia and Mercy Amba Oduyoye, ed. *With Passion and Compassion*. Maryknoll, NY: Orbis Books, 1989.

Faxon, Alicia Craig. *Women and Jesus*. Philadelphia: United Church Press, 1973.

Fernando, Chitra. "The Role of the Church in the Oppression of Women." *The Emerging Christian Woman*. S. Faria, A.V. Alexander, and J.B. Tellis-Nayak, eds. Pune, India: Salprakashan Sanchar Kendra/Ishwani Publishers, 1984.

BIBLIOGRAPHY

Fiorenza, Elisabeth Schussler. "Feminist Spirituality, Christian Identity, and Catholic Vision." *Womanspirit Rising.* Carol P. Christ and Judith Plaskow, eds. San Francisco: Harper and Row Publishers, 1979.

Gibbons, William J. ed. *Pacem in Terris.* New York: Paulist Press, 1963.

Goldsmit, Shulamit and Ernest Sweeney. "The Church and Latin American Women in Their Struggle for Equality and Justice." *Thought.* Vol. 63, No. 249 June, 1988.

Gossman, Elizabeth. "Women as Priests?" in *Apostolic Succession: Rethinking a Barrier to Unity.* Hans Kung, Concilium. Vol. 34. New York: Paulist Press, 1968.

Grana, Janice. *Images of Women in Transition.* Winona, MN: Saint Mary's Press, 1976.

Greeley, Dolores L. "Patriarchy: A Global Reality." *Where Can We Find Her? Searching for Women's Identity in the New Church.* Marie-Eloise Rosenblatt, ed. New York: Paulist Press, 1991.

Haughton, Rosemary. *The Re-Creation of Eve.* Springfield, IL: Templegate Publishers, 1985.

_____. *Song in a Strange Land.* Springfield, IL: Templegate Publishers, 1990.

Hebblethwaite, Peter. "Despite Vatican, Women on World Agenda." *National Catholic Reporter.* Kansas City, MO: June 7, 1991, p. 6.

Heyward, Carter. "Litany of the Bread." *Our Passion for Justice.* Cleveland, OH: The Pilgrim Press, 1984.

Huebsch, Bill. *A New Look at Prayer.* Mystic, CT: Twenty-Third Publications, 1991.

Jeffery, Patricia. *Frogs in a Well: Indian Women in Purdah.* New Delhi: Vikas Publishing House Pvt. Ltd., 1979.

Khan, Salma. *The Fifty Percent:Women in Development and Policy in Bangladesh.* Dhaka, Bangladesh: University Press, Ltd., 1988.

Kakwenzire, Joan. "Women and Human Rights in Uganda." *Arise.* Kampala, Uganda: Acfode Publishing Company, April-June, 1991.

Katoppo, Marianne. *Compassionate and Free.* Maryknoll, NY: Orbis Books, 1980.

Kunambi, Bernadette. "The Place of Women in the Christian Community." *African Christian Spirituality.* Aylward Shorter, ed. London: A Geoffrey Chapman book published by Cassel Ltd., 1978.

Leddy, Mary Jo. "Beyond Nagging: The Prophetic Role of Women in the Church." *Catholic New Times*. November 6, 1988.

Leege, David C. "Parish Life Among the Leaders." *Notre Dame Study of Catholic Parish Life*. Report No. 9. Notre Dame, IN: University of Notre Dame, December, 1989.

Leege, David C. and Thomas A. Trozzolo. "Participation in Catholic Parish Life: Religious Rites and Parish Activities in the 1980s." *Notre Dame Study of Catholic Parish Life*. Report No. 3. Notre Dame, IN: University of Notre Dame, December, 1984.

Lerner, Gerda. *The Creation of Patriarchy*. New York: Oxford University Press, 1986.

Matembe, Miria R.K. "The Situation of Women in Uganda." Jinja, Uganda, June 12-13, 1990.

McBrien, Richard P. "The Church of Tomorrow." *Women in Religion*. Regina Coll, ed. New York: Paulist Press, 1982.

_____. "The Feminization of Parish Ministry." Syndicated column appearing in *The Church World*. Portland, ME, August 27, 1992.

_____. "Strategies for Survival." Syndicated column appearing in *The Church World*. Portland, ME, August 20, 1992.

_____. Keynote Address, National Convention of CORPUS. Chicago, IL. June 12, 1992.

Mejia, Rodrigo, SJ. "Presence of the Lay Christians in the Preparation for the Synod of Bishops in Africa." *AFER: (African Ecclesial Review) Appeal to the African Synod*. Vol. 33, No. 4, August, 1991.

Mukamuwezi, Anna Mary, DMJ. "Church Moral Teaching and the Dignity of an African Woman." Social Justice Newsletter, No. 3, August, 1991.

Murphy, Bishop P. Francis. "Let's Start Over." *Commonweal*. September 25, 1992.

Muto, Susan. *Womanspirit*. New York: The Crossroad Publishing Company, 1991.

Nalwanga-Sebina, Abby J. and Dr. Edith R. Natukunda. "Uganda Women's Needs Assessment Survey 1988." Kampala, Uganda: Makerere University, 1988.

Okure, Teresa. "The Will to Arise: Reflections on Luke 8:40-56." *The Will to Arise*. Mercy Amba Oduyoye and Musimbi R.A. Kanyoro, eds. Maryknoll, NY: Orbis, 1992.

BIBLIOGRAPHY

"On the Dignity and Vocation of Women" *(Mulieris Dignitatem)*. Apostolic Letter, August 15, 1988.

Owanikin, Modupe. "The Priesthood of Church Women in the Nigerian Context." *The Will to Arise*. Mercy Amba Oduyoye and Musimbi R.A. Kanyoro, eds. Maryknoll, NY: Orbis, 1992.

Pavey, Constance F., ed. *The Community of Women and Men in the Church: The Sheffield Report*. Geneva: World Council of Churches, 1983.

Pax Christi. *Peacemaking: Day by Day*. Volume II. Erie, PA: Benet Press, 1989.

Perlez, Jane. "Economic Victims." *The Chicago Tribune*. April 21, 1991.

Riley, Maria. *In God's Image*. Kansas City, MO: Sheed and Ward, 1985.

Rozario, Santi. "Marginality and the cause of unmarried Christian women in a Bangladeshi village." *Contributions to Indian Sociology*. New Delhi: Sage Publications, 1986.

Ruether, Rosemary R. "Feminism and Religious Faith: Renewal or New Creation?" *Religion and Intellectual Life 3* (Winter 1986).

_____. "Motherearth and the Megamachine: A Theology of Liberation in a Feminine, Somatic and Ecological Perspective." *Womanspirit Rising*. Carol P. Christ and Judith Plaskow, eds. San Francisco: Harper and Row Publishers, 1979.

Schneiders, Sandra. *Beyond Patching: Faith and Feminism in the Catholic Church*. New York: Paulist Press, 1990.

Sewell, Marilyn. ed. "Owning Self." *Cries of the Spirit*. Boston: Beacon Press, 1991.

Stagg, Evelyn and Frank. *Women in the World of Jesus*. Philadelphia: Westminster Press, 1978.

Subbamma, Malladi. *Women, Tradition and Culture*. Dhaka: United Press, Ltd., 1985.

Swidler, Leonard. *Biblical Affirmations of Woman*. Philadelphia: Westminster Press, 1979.

Tagore, Rabindranath. *Collected Poems and Plays*. London: Macmillan, 1971.

_____. *Gitanjali*. Translated by Brother James Talarovic. Dhaka: University Press Limited, 1983.

Tamez, Elsa. *Against Machismo*. Oak Park, IL: Meyer Stone, 1987.

_____, ed. *Through Her Eyes: Women's Theology from Latin America*. Maryknoll, NY: Orbis Books, 1989.

Vidulich, Dorothy. "Sisters say new nuns group could spell trouble." *National Catholic Reporter.* Vol. 28, No. 33. Kansas City, MO, July 3, 1992.

von Wartenberg-Potter, Barbel. *We Will Not Hang Our Harps on the Willows.* Translated by Fred Kaan. Geneva: World Council of Churches, 1987.

Wabwire, Daniel. "Liberation for the African Woman." *New People.* No. 17, March-April, 1992.

Wahlberg, Rachel Conrad. *Jesus According to a Woman.* New York: Paulist Press, 1975.

Wasi, Anne Nasimiyu. "Women in the Catholic Church." *New People.* Nairobi, Kenya: Media Centre, September-October, 1991.

Weaver, Mary Jo. *New Catholic Women: A Contemporary Challenge to Traditional Religious Authority.* San Francisco: Harper and Row, 1985.

Winter, Miriam Therese. *WomanWord.* New York: The Crossroad Publishing Company, 1990.

_____. *WomanWisdom.* New York: The Crossroad Publishing Company, 1991.

_____. *WomanWitness.* New York: The Crossroad Publishing Company, 1992.

Woodward, Kenneth L. with Mary Lord. "A Sister Speaks Up." *Newsweek,* October 22, 1979.